MY MOTHER WAS VIENNESE

My Mother was Viennese

by

Peter Flatter

Copyright P Flatter © 2011

Produced by

WORDS BY DESIGN

2 South View Lodge, Piggy Lane, Bicester OX26 6HT

www.wordsbydesign.co.uk

ISBN: 978-1-4477-5587-6

To my Mother

Contents

INTRODUCTION	ix
PART I – AN EARLY LIFE REMEMBERED	1
Chapter I – The House at No 3 Mariannengasse	3
Chapter II – Before the Anschluss	11
Chapter III – After the Anschluss	25
Chapter IV – A New Life in England	31
Chapter V – The War Years	37
Chapter V – Post-War Aspirations	55
PART II – A MOTHER'S DIARY	83
Translation of Letter from Willem Van Hoogstraaten	87
A Mother's Diary	89
PART III – THE TESTIMONY	119
A Tribute	121
Chapter I – 'Eva Flatter in Haas'	123
Chapter II – Käthe Caliò, née Perlberg	131
PART IV – THE LETTERS	137
Letters From My Mother	139
Letters From Käthe Caliò	147
Letter From Tea Caliò	159
THE GUILT OF THE SURVIVOR – A POSTSCRIPT	163

INTRODUCTION

Dear Reader

May I first tell you what this book is not? It is not a biography, neither is it a history or a documentary, and its author does not pretend any literary accomplishments. But it is a serious attempt to tell the story of a mother's sacrifice and her tragic fate in the context of the historical events that marked the first half of the twentieth century. The aim in writing and compiling it was to clearly set the scene, to convey something of her person and to record the circumstances – backed by facts – that led to her cruel death.

Sadly, it has to be a story about a mother I never really got to know. I was only just 13 years of age when she sent me to safety in England and I was never to see her again. At one point I was quite sure she too would be safe; she had fled Vienna, had crossed the border into Italy and found temporary refuge with an old friend in the South Tirol – an area which had become part of Italy under the Treaty of Versailles, the Italians having fought with the Allies in WWI.

But, in WWII, when the Italians changed sides and their resistance was crumbling in the face of the Allied advance from the South, the Germans took over and it was not long before the long arm of the SS (Security Elite) and the Gestapo reached out to round up all the Jewish people in the northern provinces of Italy who, until then, had remained largely unharmed. My mother, who had struggled with loneliness, despair and abject poverty for four years, was arrested in December 1943 and eventually sent to her death in Auschwitz at the very time when the tide was turning and she would have had real hope of being re-united with her son.

That is the sad ending of a story that begins in 1925, the year of my birth, when a truncated Austria was still coming to terms with the aftermath of WWI – the loss of an empire, a ruined economy and the sacrifice of the millions who died in the fighting or perished in the Spanish influenza epidemic that followed it. Austria was not to gain stability as a democracy until after WWII, but Vienna's pre-eminence as a cultural city remained. I was made aware of this at a very early age and developed a lasting interest in the arts.

Can you imagine a little boy spending the first twelve years of his life in a 35-room 'palace' with never more than half a dozen people living there? And having a grandfather who at one time owned no less than 21 sweet shops in Vienna and was called the *Zuckerlkönig*, the King of the Sweets?

Our grandiose mansion was built in 1882 by the Kaiser's personal physician and bought by my grandfather when the physician died in the early 1900s. After WWI, its household reflected the dramatic changes the war had brought about. Only eight of the original 21 shops could be re-opened and with the family's income so drastically reduced, the full complement of servants shrunk to one housekeeper and one day-time cleaner, the cellar boilers remained unused, as did the large basement kitchen with its lift to the upper floors, and a general austerity – strictly imposed by my ever-watchful great-grandmother – descended on the household.

My life before the annexation of Austria into the Third Reich was unaffected by the political turmoil that regularly gripped the country and I was certainly not aware of the sinister threat to anyone with Jewish blood in their veins, that came with the Nazis' rise to power and Hitler's territorial ambitions.

Of course, the world changed for us completely after the Germans' jubilant entry into Austria. The persecution started from day one, and as Jews were progressively stripped of their livelihood, their property and their citizen's rights, it gradually became clear to even the most integrated of former Austrian patriots, that fleeing the country was the only viable option. The problem was where to go!

I was lucky. To get a British visa the applicant had to have a guarantor – a resident with the means to ensure that the refugee would not become a burden on the state. My father had lived in London with his second wife since 1934 and would provide the necessary guarantees.

In spite of my father abandoning her when I was three-years-old, and in spite of having to part with the son she loved more than anything else in her life, my mother did not hesitate to send me to safety. She started visa formalities immediately and then found herself confronted by obstructive tax demands from the Viennese authorities which took weeks to sort out before both my visa and an exit permit allowed me to leave for England.

My progress in becoming thoroughly anglicized only to find myself treated as an enemy alien, acquiring British citizenship and setting out with a business of my own, is all recorded in part I of this book, in which uncertainty about my mother's fate, followed by the terrible certainty that she could not have survived, runs through the pages.

As I have said, I never really got to know my mother, but the diary she kept from 1928 to 1937, although about me, reveals a lot about her. It is reproduced in the second part of this book. And letters from people who knew her, say even more and testify to the remarkable person she must have been. Compiled letters from my mother, her best friend and others, form part IV.

Part III, The Testimony, is largely based on research into the fate of Jews in Northern Italy by an Italian professor, a lady who left no stone unturned to publish the truth about the mass deportations to the extermination camps, carried out systematically by the occupying Germans. Not only did she write a book devoting a chapter to each of the victims, she was also instrumental in having a memorial erected in the centre of Arco where my mother was arrested at the end of 1943. Eva Flatter-Haas is written on the rough-hewn stone, together with the names of two other victims from the town. The fact that the memorial is the scene of a remembrance service once a year on Holocaust Memorial Day, and is attended mainly by non-

Jewish people from the town, is a touching tribute and helps to subdue a kind of self-reproach for having been spared the suffering. And whilst putting this book together has in many ways been a painful process, it has also helped me to face a feeling of guilt – the guilt of the survivor – that has been with me since I first set foot on English soil.

Finally, may I say that in describing my early life in part I of the book, I have written what I remember, or rather, how I remember. Only rarely and when really needed, have I used a little research by way of an explanation. So I hope you will overlook any unintended inaccuracies which may come to light!

Peter Flatter
Pulborough, 2011

Part I – An Early Life Remembered

Chapter I
The House at No 3 Mariannengasse

The palatial residence at number three in the Mariannengasse was built in 1882 by Kaiser Franz Josef's personal physician and was the first private house in Vienna to have running water installed. This was before taps came into general use and a small fountain in the corner of my mother's bedroom testified to the water's continuous flow.

I remember the Mariannengasse as the Harley Street of Vienna, adjacent to what was then Vienna's vast general hospital. At one end of it was the *Sanatorium Loewe* where I was born and, at the other end, the house built by the Kaiser's physician, where I grew up. I learnt later that Vienna was pre-eminent in medicine at the turn of the century and that the Mariannengasse housed many famous physicians and surgeons.

To some extent this was still the case at the time of my birth, which was 1.05am on Sunday 5th July 1925 by Caesarean Section, and is notable for the suffering and inconvenience it caused. I was one month overdue and weighed 5 Kilos. I made my mother ill for several years and stopped her from having any more children.

Number Three Mariannengasse is a listed building, but has seen some changes. Once, heavy studded outer doors opened to an archway for horse-drawn carriages. A marble staircase led to the first floor landing and continued in three flights to the second floor – all brilliantly lit by a glass roof. A separate staircase served a third floor where guest rooms and servants' quarters used to be located.

Nowadays, it has become the headquarters of the *Wiener Elektrizitätswerke*, with a glazed main entrance and an extra top floor, also mainly glass.

In my time at number three, the basement housed a big unused kitchen with a lift serving both floors. There was also a scullery, a laundry and a gymnasium, of which I made frequent, if half-hearted use. Further down in the cellar, a boiler had provided central heating before the First World War and a large empty coal cellar was once replenished through pavement manholes. The house was built to stay warm during the long freezing winters. All rooms had radiators hidden behind elaborate grills, and double windows, separated by a heavy draft-reducing bolster, kept out the cold and noise.

The first floor opened out to a veranda with steps leading down to a large garden. It was reached through a windowless smoking room with red plush seating and a glass showcase displaying amongst other treasures a *Kaisersemmel*, the very first white bread roll triumphantly purchased after the First World War. It was rock-hard and I would often admire it with awe.

A spacious dining room adjoined the smoking room. This had a secret door in its oak panelling which opened to a staircase leading to a bedroom on the second floor. According to well-founded family gossip, a paternal uncle frequently used the staircase to visit my maternal grandmother. You see, my father and my mother were first cousins.

A door in the dining room led to my mother's large bed-sitting room, which must previously have been the physician's consulting room. It was on two levels and notable for three things: the heavy velvet curtain surrounding my mother's bed, the fact that my bed was there too, and the little marble fountain in the corner. Another feature was a heavy wrought-iron grill guarding the large central window overlooking the garden. Every night before going to bed, my mother stood me in the open window in front of the grill to breathe the fresh scented air.

The velvet curtain hiding my mother's bed during the day had another function. When my behaviour had become quite insufferable and my mother was showing signs of desperation, I would offer to go behind the curtain for five minutes or so and then emerge transformed into a good boy cleansed of all my wickedness. Needless to say, my mother went along with this ruse, if only to enjoy a (albeit short) period of affection and model behaviour.

Not only did I sleep in my mother's bedroom, I expected her to be there with me after I had gone to bed. My tantrums must have been unbearable on the few evenings she did go out. But little did she know that when she had gone, I would connect an old crystal radio set to a bell wire, put on the earphones and search for signals. Beaminster was the long-wave station that came up most frequently, but it was of little use to me as I could not understand a word of English.

The other side of the bed-sitting room led to what had once been just a corridor. To provide self-contained facilities for the Flatter family within the original Haas household, the corridor had been converted into a small curtained-off bathroom on one side and a series of cupboards and wardrobes on the other. Hair washing tantrums dominate my memory of the bathroom. My mother had great difficulty in persuading me to submit to this greatly feared procedure, which included rubbing egg yolk into my scalp

As you have now gathered, I was a difficult child. Looking back, I deeply regret having caused my mother much pain during the relatively short time we were together. What makes it worse is the frustration of having only a vague memory of her – I have tried so desperately to remember her more clearly!

The corridor also provided access to the oak-panelled billiard room which doubled as a library. I have fond memories of this room because of its wonderful smell – the smell of print. I would often go in just to savour its fragrance – my mother sometimes suggested I did so! The windows overlooked the street, as did the windows of the last room on the first floor, the pink salon with its elaborate cut-glass chandelier. But the billiard room remains notable for an occasion when it was covered in white sheets and transformed into an emergency operating theatre on my behalf. A gland under my right jaw had turned septic and was producing a sack of pus which got bigger every day. The resulting fever was so severe that the doctors decided not to move me. Instead I had to spend hours each day in a tunnel heated by rows of light bulbs to 'ripen' the sack. About half a pint of pus was eventually drained from it. No anaesthetic was necessary for the incision; I was too far gone to feel anything. I suppose nowadays a course of antibiotics would have cured me in a few days.

After this and other more normal childhood illnesses, I always looked forward to the period of convalescence that followed. I would be pampered and thoroughly spoilt by my grandmother, who insisted that I should be given special delicacies to speed my recovery. One of these was called *Schodo* and consisted of egg yolks beaten into a delicious frothy desert over boiling water with a little sweet wine and sugar – the equivalent of an Italian *Zabaione*. As I progressed, my grandmother would even feed me on caviar, presumably in the belief that anything so expensive was bound to be highly beneficial.

It was not long before I discovered that the caviar came from a cupboard located behind the upstairs door of the secret staircase and that I too could reach it from the dining room below. It was full of expensive food items, which obviously needed to be hidden from the rest of the household, especially from my great-grandmother who, as we shall see, was very partial to rich food.

Half-way up the marble staircase to the second floor, a servant's day room had been converted into a kitchen during the Great War and had become the stronghold of the formidable Mitzi, our cook. You should have seen her tackling a live, slithery carp with a rolling pin! I spent hours watching her and have loved cooking ever since.

The second floor started with my maternal uncle's bedroom, then led to my grandmother's bed-sitting room complete with baby grand piano (she was a piano teacher), and continued to a large boudoir-cum-washroom with balcony, all on the garden side. Crossing a corridor and a bathroom with just a bath and a gas ring, one came to my great-grandmother's bedroom, followed by my maternal aunt's bedroom, a large sitting room with a beautiful tiled stove, and then to my grandfather's bedroom – all facing the street. To connect back to my uncle's room on the garden side of the house, there was a long larder kept under lock and key by my great-grandmother. The larder always had a pungent smell, a mixture of washing soap and cheese. The soap was kept on a shelf and only released for use when it had hardened and would last longer. The cheese was *Harzer* made by the old lady – an incredibly strong cheese made from strained soured milk, which seemed to mature to runny perfection on the dusty shelves.

Another of my great-grandmother's specialities was to secretly boil half a pig's head on the little gas ring in the upstairs bathroom next to her bedroom and eat it all on her own. In consequence, she had somewhat turbulent insides and seemed at times to be propelling herself along.

I too could indulge my robust appetite on the second floor. In the corridor from the landing to the washroom on one side and the piggy bathroom on the other, there was a lift from the old basement kitchens and, opposite, a cupboard where a huge round *Ankerbrot* sour-dough rye loaf was kept with a large bread knife, some butter, salt and a butter knife. The idea was to cut a thick, horseshoe shaped slice, spread it generously with butter, sprinkle it with coarse salt and cut it into mouth-watering, finger-sized pieces. I don't know why it was there and I am sure it was not intended for me, but I can still smell and taste that wonderful bread – the antithesis of today's cotton wool!

The bread was made by the *Anker* bakery in Vienna and must have commanded some 90% of the market there. Recently, I met members of the Vienna Piano Trio who were on a tour of the UK. It emerged that the pianist was the grandson of the owners of the bakery. He told me that they lost the business and eventually their lives after the annexation of Austria into the German Reich.

As a young innocent I did not realise that the rooms of my grandmother and her son revealed secrets about their respective sex lives. Being inquisitive by nature, I had found quite a number of strange rubber objects in one of the drawers of my uncle's desk – left there since he had left to marry his Moravian beauty many years earlier. Of course, I experimented to discover the purpose of these mysterious elastic objects, but I had to wait for 'enlightenment' to change my impression of an uncle who had always treated me with rather pompous severity.

My grandmother's uncorroborated secret was more subtle. We have already heard the allegation of clandestine visits by Richard, my paternal uncle, using the staircase which spiralled up to her bedroom from the dining room below. Well, I was told that she was never to be disturbed, even when she was not playing the piano, so with no-one in adjoining rooms and padded, double, main doors into her room, any secret trysts would certainly have remained undiscovered, at least by those who were not supposed to know.

My playground was the large garden at the back of the house. There was a sandpit which I soon outgrew; there were trees to climb and bushes to hide in, a highly productive walnut tree and lots and lots of beautiful lilies bordering the flower beds. At the end of the garden facing our house, was a five-storey apartment block which also belonged to my grandparents. It had a dyers and cleaners on the ground floor, run by the Epstein family who lived above the shop. The Epsteins were distantly related to my father's family and the daughter, Else, a tubby, cheerful lady, was a frequent visitor at my paternal grandparents' house in the Wintergasse. There she had fallen in love with my uncle, Richard – another conquest on his part – but was too timid to tell him how she felt.

Sadly, old man Epstein was suffering from advanced Parkinson's disease. His frail, pale, unshaven appearance in pyjamas made a frightening impression on my one and only visit to the flat above the shop. It was the first time I had come face to face with approaching death. Eventually, Else Epstein too became a tragic figure. After fleeing Austria to escape the Nazis, she committed suicide.

One of the two apartments on the top floor was occupied by the family of my maternal uncle Benno, with Mimi his Moravian wife and their two daughters, Ditta and Gerda. This uncle was the black sheep of the family, but not because he had chosen to be baptised before marrying his Catholic bride. To escape his debts and charges of embezzlement, he had left Austria before the annexation and had joined the French Foreign Legion. Aunt Mimi was left to struggle on her own, initially with some help from my grandmother. She was a very handsome, courageous and astute woman and I believe she survived the war and immediate post-war years by entertaining first German and later Russian Officers and by the debt of gratitude owed her by a wealthy Jewish friend, whom she hid from the Nazis throughout the war – an astonishing feat!

During the war, my aunt also had to come to terms with the loss of her older daughter, Ditta, who died of scarlet fever. Gerda, my younger cousin, survived the war but not before she had been raped by Russian soldiers who went on the rampage for three days after heavy street battles to occupy Vienna.

Towards the end of the war, uncle Benno turned up in Yugoslavia with the Allies as a broadcaster of war propaganda intended to demoralise the German fighting forces. When he returned to Vienna, Aunt Mimi took him back. The unfortunate man subsequently embarked on a number of unsuccessful business ventures before dieing of leukaemia at the age of only 56.

The garden was more or less square and there were large apartment blocks (not belonging to us) on either side. Some had windowless walls; two of them overlooked the garden. I was never aware of anyone watching me, but one boy about my age did. His name was Fritz Thielberg and we became very good friends until we were separated by events.

But let us consider how my family got to possess the physician's palatial house with its beautiful large garden – a unique feature in central Vienna. I was told it began with my maternal grandfather setting out on foot from his Moravian home with the proverbial golden Gulden in his pocket, to seek his fortune in the great capital of the Austro-Hungarian Empire. He was soon apprenticed to a confectioner and, after a spell of shop-sweeping, began rapidly to climb the shopkeeper's ladder until he had not one, but twenty-one confectioners' shops and became known in Vienna as *Zuckerlkönig* – King of the Sweets.

When the Kaiser's physician died, my grandfather bought the house and the family lived there in style until 1914, when the Great War forced the closure of most of the shops. The business recovered somewhat after the war, but only to a total of eight outlets, so that even long before my grandfather became ill with liver cancer in 1934, the household had to be slimmed down dramatically to consist only of a live-in cook and a daytime maid.

From time to time, I would hear about the Great War and the terrible deprivation suffered by the population. There were lots of stories of the Viennese going out to the farms in the country to exchange precious possessions for desperately needed food. The most extreme example was that of a chicken purchased with a grand piano! There was no flour and the nearest to bread was a loaf made from *Wruken*, a kind of swede normally used as animal feed. Cakes, I was told, were made with cooked and mashed chestnuts.

The war seriously disrupted my father's studies at the Vienna Academy where he was training to become a portrait painter. Like many Jewish young men anxious to defend what they regarded as their fatherland, he volunteered for the army and fought as a second lieutenant in the *Kaiserjäger* regiment on the Italian front, where he was twice wounded by gunfire. He told me that the Italians avoided close combat and that there was little movement by the opposing armies in the mountainous terrain of the Dolomites.

At the time of my birth in 1925, Austrians were still trying to come to terms with the Treaty of Versailles; an empire lost and replaced by a small, unstable republic, plagued by political turmoil and bankruptcy.

Chapter II
Before the Anschluss

Listing the occupants of Number Three, we have accounted for two maternal grandparents, a great-grandmother, a mother, her son and the two servants.

So where was my father?

At the time of his marriage in 1924 to Eva Haas, Otto Flatter was a penniless portrait painter, forced to accept the hospitality of his in-laws in the Mariannengasse. This perceived humiliation, together with an ailing wife after my birth and my refusal to stop screaming by day and night, seems to have been too much for him. He began to seek and find consolation in the arms of Hilda Loewe, a glamorous concert pianist and composer of popular hit tunes. Hilda composed under the pseudonym of Henry Love in the 1920s and '30s, when pop music openly written by a woman would not have succeeded.

As a young and beautiful pianist Hilda must have made quite an impression on the Viennese concert public. During WWI she entertained the troops, and was to do it again with ENSA in WWII. Once, on a camouflaged troop ship sailing down the Adriatic in moonlight, she was asked to parade up and down on deck in her long flowing white dress to persuade the enemy that this really was a hospital ship! For a time she was engaged to a student of Sigmund Freud, but it seems that the young man was practising too much psychoanalysis on himself; he became depressed and killed himself.

By the time I was three, my father started to stay away from home, and before long my parents had divorced. Eventually I was to see my father only once every second weekend. The divorce caused a permanent rift between him and his lawyer brother, because Richard represented my mother in the legal proceedings in which my father was the guilty party. They never spoke again, even though my uncle managed to get to England in 1939.

Like my father, Uncle Richard was interned at the outbreak of war, but instead of being sent to the Isle of Man, he was shipped to Australia. After spending six weeks in the hull of a ship in submarine-infested waters, my poor uncle was sent back to suffer the same nightmare voyage again. His health never fully recovered and it was little consolation to him that the authorities regretted having subjected genuine refugees from Nazi Germany to this ordeal.

One photograph from the time of the divorce shows me walking hand in hand with my governess, Frau Marie, and another sitting on my great-grandmother's lap in the garden. I am wearing a skirt in both pictures – *de rigueur* for three-year-old boys in those days – and displaying a large mop of platinum curls.

It was also at this time that my mother began writing a diary which would record seven years of my life – what I said, what I did and how she felt about it all. It shows her to be a deeply caring mother, but also an uncompromising judge of the strengths and weaknesses of my character as it developed. That the diary survived the terrible events that were to unfold is due entirely to my mother's foresight. It came quite unexpectedly into my possession in 1946 and it did help me to get to know her a little better.

When I reached the age of four, my mother's health had improved sufficiently to stimulate an urge for change. So we set off on a grand European tour of which I particularly remember three events: having my character analysed at an institute for psychology in Stuttgart and opting for orange when asked to choose a colour; being lifted and hugged by an over-zealous customer in a Paris shop and hating it; and thirdly, seeing a little Dutch girl do what most little Dutch peasant girls did in those days – walk securely under the traditional long skirt of her mother.

In Holland I was also thrilled by a visit to one of the large transatlantic liners waiting to depart. It seemed that one minute we were walking inside the terminal building and the next we had emerged from a corridor into a vast floating hotel with stewards rushing about in all directions. I guess we must have been seeing someone off, because we were soon asked to disembark.

By the time I was five we were in Italy to spend six months in Merano in the South Tirol, by then called the Alto Adige and lost to Austria as part of the Treaty of Versailles. The mixture of old Austria and modern Italy gave the town a very special, altogether inviting atmosphere. We stayed *en pension* in very simple accommodation. As my grandmother could no longer afford to fully support us, my mother worked in a shop selling costume jewellery to eek out her shrinking allowance. I had a playmate my own age at the pension and apparently picked up quite a lot of Italian. I vividly remember the daily lunch in the bare, bright dining room – it was almost always Spaghetti Napolitano and a gorgeous fresh lettuce and tomato salad. It was there that I learnt never to dress a green salad with anything other than good olive oil and lemon juice.

A photograph of me standing with my mother by the railings bordering the river Adige in Meran in 1930 is now on the title page of a book by an Italian professor, recording the fate suffered by Jews in Northern Italy in 1943/4, after the Germans had moved in.

I was, of course, too young to be aware of the injustice suffered by the Tirolese people under Benito Mussolini, who systematically forced farmers off their land and colonised the area with Italians from the South. However, Merano still gave the impression of an imperial spa town with its grand *Kurhaus*, its luxury hotels, its fabulous patisseries and its wealthy clientele. No wonder my mother decided to settle there for a few months, while my father fumed that the boy was not getting an education.

In actual fact, my mother taught me to read and write while we were there. When I joined the elementary school in Vienna at the end of 1931, I was well ahead of other pupils.

My time at school in Vienna came to an end in 1934 when my grandfather took to his bed and began to suffer agonies from the liver cancer that would slowly kill him. The atmosphere in the house changed with the cries of pain and the nursing activities; hardly the right environment for a nine-year-old boy. So it was decided to send me to what was probably the only boarding school known in Austria at the time, the *Landeserziehungsheim Grinzing*.

This establishment, in the well-preserved wine village of Grinzing in the outskirts of Vienna, catered for boys from the age of ten, so I was just too young to have lessons there. I became a boarder and attended the local elementary school a few minutes down the road. Needless to say, I learnt a lot at a very tender age from the older boarders about sex and drugs. In particular, I remember the son of a wealthy Bulgarian, who seemed to have an unlimited supply of opium cigarettes which he generously shared with his fellow pupils. Luckily, I did not like the taste.

We were very conscientiously looked after. During the winter, the matron would come to the dormitories at bedtime to anoint our legs with glycerine. Winters were fierce and knees highly vulnerable to frostbite. I also remember that the boarding school had a magnificent model railway which spanned three rooms and provided endless fascination.

It was whilst attending the Grinzing elementary school that I fell in love for the first time. The object of my desire was the pretty eight-year-old daughter of an actress. As she reciprocated my feelings, we sealed our love by 'spending pennies' together on the same side of the woodland path which should have separated the boys from the girls during a school outing 'comfort stop'.

It was also at the *Landeserziehungsheim* that I experienced warfare for the first time. Behind us were the hills of the Vienna Woods, vantage points from which the Austrian army bombarded the *Karl-Marx-Hof*, a huge block of workers' flats and a model of social housing, which had become the stronghold of rebellious socialists and communists. The last time I saw the building, the scars of the bombardment were still there. Of course, we youngsters quite enjoyed the sound of the shells whistling overhead and the noise of the explosions on their departure and arrival.

In the turbulent times between the wars, incidents from suppressed political parties, that would today be called acts of terrorism, were commonplace, and I witnessed what was perhaps the most spectacular of these, undoubtedly perpetrated by Austrian members of the National Socialist party. I was in the *Prater*, the extensive open parkland of which the famous funfair is part, when I saw several fire engines racing in the direction of the *Rotunde*, Vienna's main exhibition building, named after its round, domed middle section.

Quite a crowd had already gathered when I got there. Flames were spurting out of the centre of the dome which was supported by a central column. It appeared that arsonists had set fire to the base of the column and the flames had reached the top. To the amazement of onlookers, two firemen with hoses started to climb the roof from the edge to the centre to reach the flames. Hardly had they got there when the entire roof collapsed, plunging the hapless men to their deaths.

By this time it seemed as though half of the population of Vienna had arrived and wanted to get as close a look as possible, so that the people nearest the burning building were getting pushed dangerously close. Luckily, mounted police arrived and drove the whole crowd back out of danger. The heat was quite incredible. As the fire took hold of the whole building, even the steel girders burned with white heat, and such was the scale of the inferno that the fire continued for several days. Crowds of Viennese, myself included, trekked up the hills overlooking Vienna to see the glow at night – still spectacular for at least seven days.

Of course, the *Prater* was best known for its funfair and especially for the 61 metre giant ferris wheel, a landmark at the entrance to the park. It was constructed by two British engineers and created a sensation when it was erected in 1897 to mark the 50th jubilee of

Emperor Franz Josef's reign. Today it would be dwarfed by the London Eye with its 135 metre diameter.

A welcoming smell of sizzling sausages greeted the visitors to the funfair. Whenever I had enough pocket money, I would buy *Ein Paar Frankfurters* which came on a cardboard tray with a bread roll and a large dollop of mild continental mustard. These sausages, which were joined at one end, were rather perversely named - in Frankfurt and elsewhere in Germany they were called *Wienerli*.

A large number of shows competed for customers by promising amazing revelations. The most popular seemed to be those offering freaks of one kind or another. The tallest or the fattest or the most bearded woman 'in the world' would be on display inside and postcards would be for sale revealing them in the nude (as we were told we would want to see them) when held up to the light. Another attraction was the faked near-electrocution of a man whose quaking body was supposed to be subjected to ever-higher voltages.

After my grandfather died in 1935, I had remained in Grinzing long enough to go straight into secondary school education in Vienna. At the time there were three choices: the Gymnasium which provided a highly academic curriculum, the *Realschule* which concentrated on practical subjects and a half-way house, the Real-Gymnasium. As I was not particularly good with facts and figures, I was sent to a *Realschule*, a boys-only school in the Glasergasse near the Danube Canal, where I achieved some distinction in subjects such as Geometry and Biology before my schooling there came to an abrupt end in the spring of 1938.

It took about 45 minutes each way to the school and back. I would have my satchel strapped to my back and would usually walk alone. I remember stopping quite often in front of an antique shop before crossing the Währingerstrasse. It had a portrait of Christ in the window. The intriguing feature of this picture was the eyes; at first they seemed closed, but after staring at the face for a little while they appeared to open and look at the viewer.

I was also intrigued by the horsemeat butcher I passed before getting to the school. He had all the sausages and joints that another butcher opposite displayed, but his meat was almost half the price and must have been a great boon to the poor.

The Glasergasse led directly to the quayside of the *Donaukanal*, the tributary of the Danube, so often mistaken for the great river itself. Underneath the road was one of Vienna's main sewers discharging effluent into the canal. For the boys from the *Realschule* it was a great favourite for clandestine exploration and it was later to feature prominently in the film 'The Third Man'. The sewer was quite easily accessible from the canal embankment and, because of its size, was constructed like a surface canal complete with a wide towpath.

My time back home in the Mariannengasse before the annexation was the last I spent with my mother. Sunday was the only free day as school did not finish until one or two o'clock on Saturdays. Sunday outings alternated between excursions with my mother, usually into the Vienna Woods, and trips with my father to his parental home in the Wintergasse or to his sister's in Klosterneuburg.

Klosterneuburg is an attractive town on the Danube, a short stretch upstream from Vienna. My uncle-by-marriage, Arthur Graumann, was a lawyer who worked for a large international insurance company in the city. He and my aunt had two boys, Bobby my age and Hans two years older. They lived in a house on the hillside overlooking the river and old Klosterneuburg with its famous monastery, the *Stift*. Their house was built on a slope and had a garage in the basement. It looked like a typical suburban dwelling in England looks today. In the garage was a *Steyr 120* – a car similar in shape to the Volkswagen designed by Porsche in 1933. Running a car was an impressive achievement in Austria in those days. Unfortunately, I could not enjoy this luxurious form of transport – I felt sick almost as soon as I got in.

Visits to the Graumanns were always marked by some form of entertainment. My aunt, who had a beautiful contralto voice, would sing, accompanied on the piano by 'Aunt Hilda', later to become my stepmother. Uncle Arthur played the cello and he too would give a recital with Hilda at the piano. There were also parlour games galore, but the undoubted favourite was a performance of the *Puppentheater*.

This was a very sophisticated puppet theatre entirely created by the adults. The storyline and script was a combined effort and always dealt with the strange adventures of myself and Bobby, my cousin, also born in 1925. My father painted the scenery and the characters and wrote most of the lyrics, which Hilda then set to music. These highly professional performances always amused the adults as much as the children and were also enjoyed by friends and neighbours.

Bobby's brother, my cousin Hans, was two years older and a mathematical child prodigy. His ability to do huge sums in his head was really astonishing and he eventually became a senior statistician with WHO, the United Nations' World Health Organisation. Sadly he suffered a heart attack in America in his late forties and died, leaving his wife to bring up their two children on her own.

Bobby, on the other hand, lived to 84, after spending his last years in the South of France in retirement from a successful career with the United Nations in Geneva.

Other fortnightly outings with my father were spent at his parents' house in the Wintergasse, which was located in the north-western part of Vienna. This still had the appearance of a rural village street, going back to the days when farmers drove through with their produce in the very early hours of the morning. Many of them would stop off at my grandfather's liquor store to warm up with a quick home-distilled Schnapps before setting off to the central markets.

Sigmund Flatter was no longer alive at the time of my visits, but the shop was still selling spirits, and a redundant brandy distillery was still there for me to investigate. I was told that my grandfather had to get up at four in the morning to prepare for the customers who would arrive from five o'clock onwards.

A number of things stand out from my recollections of the Wintergasse. There was *Anook*, the Alsatian, sadly on a chain in the little courtyard behind the house, but greatly loved and eventually sadly missed by the whole family. There was the family joke of my grandmother offering visitors a *Schnitzel* when she didn't have one to offer. And although it was a modest household, there was a cook to watch and it was there that I learnt how to make a genuine Viennese *Apfelstrudel*, the dough gently stretched into translucent paper thickness over a flour-dusted table cloth covering the kitchen table.

The reader will have gathered by now that I was a precocious little glutton when it came to food. I was always hungry and one of my regular haunts was the *Automatenbuffet,* a futuristic type of self-service snack bar, where open sandwiches, pastries and drinks were dispensed automatically. Covered turntables would rotate when money was inserted to make the item of choice accessible. Drinks emerged from spouts in the wall and there was even a glass-washing water jet.

The *Automatenbuffet* I frequented was close by in the Alserstrasse. I could get to it in a couple of minutes through our garden and the driveway of our apartment block. It had a choice of sandwiches costing from thirty to a mere ten Groschen – probably the equivalent of one penny at that time. Thirty Groschen produced a very posh sandwich, piled high with egg, salami, ham and gurkin, whereas the 10 Groschen version had only a grated carrot mayonnaise on it. I was often hard up and had to make do with the carrot topping.

My interest in food also came to the fore when preparing for Sunday excursions with my mother. Money was tighter still by the time I was allowed to take charge of supplies and I prided myself on providing ample sustenance on a very low budget. For a few coppers one could buy a packet of *Gänsegrammeln* (delicious goose chitterlings), or ten dekagrams of charcuterie off-cuts in a *Papierstanitzel* (a neatly twisted paper bag) – to be eaten with a pickled cucumber and crusty roll.

As I said, money was tight. With only a few sweet shops remaining, and my grandfather no longer there to run them, my grandmother was struggling to give my mother an adequate allowance. As a result I was often left to wait outside the *Dorotheum* – Vienna's large state-run pawn shop – whilst my mother borrowed what she could get from the few items of jewellery and the two fur coats she possessed. Sadly, I do not remember ever going there to retrieve any items.

Next to the *Dorotheum* was a restaurant with a window that displayed, amongst other culinary exhibits, a monstrously large goose liver preserved in liquid in a huge glass jar. To emphasise the size of this grotesque piece of offal, the remaining internal organs had been left attached and appeared tiny, totally dwarfed by the highly prized *foie gras*. Of course, I was made aware of the cruelty of stuffing maize down a goose's throat, which also involved stroking its neck to make room for more. The farmers got good money for geese with large livers and refuted accusations of cruelty by claiming that the animals enjoyed the experience and were eager for more.

But back to the Sunday excursions. The proximity of the Vienna Woods meant that one could be engulfed by beautiful woodland within minutes of getting off the tram at its terminus. There always had to be an *Ausflugsziel* – a destination to aim for – perhaps a vantage point affording rewarding views or a *Jausenstation* – literally an afternoon tea station – where one could buy drinks and was allowed to eat one's own food. On a warm day, my mother would recommend hot tea and I discovered to my surprise that it was a much more effective thirst-quencher than ice-cold drinks, of which *Soda-Himbeer,* raspberry cordial mixed with soda water, was my favourite.

My interest in food also led me to what was not quite the red-light district of Vienna, but was nevertheless a street considered unsuitable for children after dark. This was the Griechengasse where painted ladies in short skirts seemed to me to have nothing to do but stand in doorways. In this street there opened a large state-of-the-art takeaway fish and chip shop, in layout reminiscent of today's burger palaces.

On entering this innovation, one was given a card which was perforated at the serving stations with the purchases made. At the checkout, the card was inserted into a machine and automatically produced the bill. Although I stuck my nose into this place quite often, I never bought anything, as my main meals were provided for.

Nearby was an area where down-and-outs gathered. As there was no state social security, tramps, beggars and the very poor were entirely dependent on charity in some form to stay alive. Vienna was full of beggars, some genuinely disabled, others pretending to be blind or mad or even leg-less. There were several disreputable-looking women with red hair carrying dolls to signify their madness, and I particularly remember a 'blind' man next to the entrance of the huge *Allgemeine Krankenhaus* – Vienna's general hospital – who had a raven tied to a perch. In exchange for money, the bird would randomly pick an envelope predicting the donor's future.

Food was not my only passion. I developed an early fascination for operetta, thanks to what was then the *Stadtteater* in the Skodagasse close by. One of Vienna's grand venues before WWI, the theatre was reduced to cut-price performances local people could afford. There it cost very little to see the masterpieces of Franz Lehar and Johann Strauss and my great favourite, 'The White Horse Inn'. I just loved everything about this piece: the setting, the music and a story imbued with typically Viennese nostalgia. It became a national showpiece and, eventually, the most frequently performed musical in the world.

Some time in 1937, I decided to teach myself to cycle. Where the bicycle came from, I have no idea. It was a heavy old thing with a useless front brake and a push-back-pedal rear brake. My first attempt in a country lane began well enough and I was congratulating myself on having mastered balance and steering, when I realised I also had to stop. The saddle was far too high for my feet to touch the ground and the more I slowed the more I wobbled; there was nothing for it – I threw myself into the ditch and crawled out much the worse from nettle stings.

I never knew how many or what kind of friends my mother had. Although she was quite active as a writer and also had me to look after, I think she associated with some revolutionaries and also with a generation of highly educated young ladies, who were unable or unwilling to put their qualifications to full use, and instead joined different movements and followed transient exotic cults.

Anyway, when I was learning to ride a bicycle, my mother produced a middle-aged gentleman who was asked to cycle with me in town traffic. Again, everything went well until I got the front tyre caught in a tram rail and caused quite a hold-up, escaping with minor bruising.

Another friend of my mother's probably belonged to the outlawed socialist or communist party. He must have felt vulnerable because he entrusted a revolver into my mother's care, which she promptly hid in my, by then, redundant toy drawer. But that was not the end of it; a few weeks later she received another gun from him. It was the real thing this time; the first gun had been a toy – a replica to test her dependability.

On one occasion she had a very good-looking visitor with greying hair and a gentle manner. I was asked to show him out and he took his leave by kissing me, causing embarrassment if not revulsion. I found out later that his name was Willem van Hoogstraden, an eminent conductor and music director of the Stuttgart Symphony Orchestra, who had known my mother since she was in her late teens. His name turns up again after the war in part two of this book.

But I must not forget Käthe Perlberg, my mother's close friend from student days. She lived with her parents and sister in a luxurious apartment on the Kochplatz, a square off the Ringstrasse near the Danube Canal. I only remember visiting there once and meeting Lilly, Käthe's younger sister, who apparently suffered from epilepsy – an illness I did not understand at the time.

Well before the Annexation, Käthe had fallen in love with a consumptive Italian street musician. He was an older man – a fine violinist who could no longer find regular work. They married and

Käthe left Austria for good. Later she would provide shelter for my fugitive mother.

By the end of 1934, the Austrian National Socialist Party was gaining ground by the day. The diminutive Austrian dictator, Dr Dolfuss, had banned the Nazis in 1933. He was subsequently murdered by them in July 1934, but not before he had ruthlessly put down an uprising by the Socialists in February of that year, in what amounted to civil war. Hitler's pressure on Dollfuss' successor, Dr Schuschnigg, to make Austria a puppet state ready for incorporation into a greater Germany, was growing relentlessly. Over the next three years Schuschnigg fought hard to suppress the Nazi party and to maintain Austrian independence. I remember the rallying song aimed at Austrian youth at the time; here it is with a literal translation:

Ihr Jungen schliesst die Reihen gut	You youngsters, close ranks tightly
Ein Todter fuehrt euch an	A dead man leads you on
Er gab fuer Oesterreich sein Blut	He gave his blood for Austria
Ein wahrer deutscher Mann.	A true German man.
Die Mörderkugel die ihn traf	The murder bullet that hit him
Sie riss das Volk aus Zank und Schlaf.	Pulled the people out of strife and sleep.
Ihr Jungen steht bereit	You youngsters, stand ready
Mit Dollfuss in die neue Zeit!	With Dollfuss into a new era.

But the effect of years of instability and the pressure from outside and inside the country was too great – ultimately some 99% of those who were persuaded to vote in a referendum wanted the Anschluss with Germany. Schuschnigg finally gave up in March 1938, leaving the way clear for a triumphant 'Reunification'.

The first German troops were welcomed by a jubilant population on Saturday 12th of March and exultant crowds greeted Hitler on his way into Vienna the following week. I am sure that many of those cheering had marched on the Ringstrasse a few days earlier shouting: *"Rot-Weiss-Rot bis zum Todt"* – a pledge to defend the Austrian flag to the death!

Chapter III
After the Anschluss

When I try to describe the tidal wave of violent anti-Semitism that instantly swept through what had been Austria, I can only think of the Senator McCarthy anti-communist era in the United States, as a very inadequate example of the hysterical witch-hunt for anyone with Jewish blood in their veins.

Overnight, staff handed in their notices to Jewish employers, only to get their jobs back and more as soon as the business was 'aryanised'. Our two servants left us within a week; Anna went in spiteful mood, but Mitzi, who had been part of the household since the time of my birth, cried bitter tears. She had no alternative but to go and she went without knowing that the house would soon see other occupants.

It was also not long before the 'Umschulung' began; Jewish children were transferred to segregated schools, where non-Jewish teachers predictably protested at having to teach them and where contingents of Hitler Youth waited outside to beat them up.

I was, of course, not spared this treatment. I was moved from the Realschule in the Glasergasse to a school in the Schottengasse and given some haphazard lessons. Luckily, this did not last more than two months. The summer vacation saw me sent out into the country with my two girl cousins and a good time was had by all, despite the huge banner at the railway station proclaiming 'Juden betreten diesen Ort auf ihre eigene Gefahr' – Jews enter this village at their peril! I did, in fact, take big risks, like giving the 'Heil Hitler' salute in the local pub every time I fetched some beer for the girls' governess who, obligingly, was less observant after a pint or two. Without the 'Heil Hitler', I would have been closely scrutinized and would not have been served, but if my Jewish origins had been discovered my 'Heil' would have been my downfall!

My cousins too, were at risk. They would not have passed as 'racially pure' under the notorious Nuremberg laws. Two Aryan grandparents and a baptised father would not have saved them from persecution. But with my uncle away in the French foreign legion, my Aunt Mimi, their resourceful mother, was able to protect them. What a tragedy that the elder died of scarlet fever during the war!

I had incurred a similar but less serious risk when visiting cinemas, all of which displayed a prominent notice: 'Juden ist der Eintritt verboten' – Jews are prohibited from entering. Not yet thirteen-years-old, I went to every U-film shown in Vienna between March and my departure into the countryside. It was the only escape from the upheaval dominating life in the Mariannengasse.

One day probably in early June, two smartly uniformed SS-Officers had called at the house, clicked their heels in front of my mother and told her that they were taking the building over in two weeks time as an SS headquarter. No alternative accommodation or compensation was offered. Where my poor mother, grandmother and great-grandmother went, I do not know, because I had already been sent into the country and left Austria directly from there.

I did, of course, witness many of the well-documented outrages committed against Jews during the paranoia that swept Vienna immediately after the Annexation: Jews on their knees scrubbing the pavements to remove the insignia of the old dictatorship, the Kruppenkreuz, whilst crowds jeered and kicked and spat at them; a Jew being knifed to death on what is now called the Friedensbruecke – the bridge of peace; Jewish shopkeepers made to sit in their own shop windows wearing a notice such as 'I am a Jewish swine'; and perhaps worst of all, the yellow star soon to be worn by all adults when out, and the revulsion and abuse meted out to its wearers in buses, trams and other public places.

I also clearly remember the profound disbelief with which these terrible events were met by those around me. My relatives and their friends had all become fully assimilated into Viennese life, often to the point of denying their origins. They saw themselves as German Austrians first and foremost. "Had they not contributed massively to the culture, sciences and economic development of the country and had they not fought as patriots in the First World War?" They wanted to believe that the explosion of violent anti-Semitism was simply a reaction following many relatively trouble-free years, and that it would soon burn itself out.

Jews in Vienna had chosen baptism to try to avoid discrimination, well into the previous century. Gustav Mahler became a Christian because, as a Jew, he could not have become music director of the imperial court orchestra. However, Emperor Franz Josef was known to have befriended Jews and defended them publicly. Now, with anti-Semitism rife among the people of Austria, it only needed the Nazis to whip up their prejudices into a frenzy of hatred and violence.

My mother had registered me as 'konfessionslos' on my birth certificate. She felt that I should not have any religion selected for me until I was old enough to decide for myself. In the event, I stayed 'konfessionslos' and looked to nature and especially the mystery of the universe for spiritual inspiration. I am sure my Uncle Benno's conversion to Roman Catholicism was pragmatically and not spiritually driven. He converted before marrying his Roman Catholic beauty from Moravia, and their children were brought up as practising Christians.

There was not a trace of Jewishness in the Mariannengasse. We observed all the Christian festivals. I would find my presents under a lovingly decorated tree on Christmas Eve. We ate fish that evening, usually carp, and on several occasions my mother took me to midnight mass to enjoy the spectacle and to experience the atmosphere of awe and devotion.

We also celebrated New Year's Eve with suckling pig, funny hats and crackers. The crackers always contained good luck charms and forecast highly optimistic good fortunes, but we had our own special way of peering into the future. Melting lead in a metal ladle and tipping it into cold water produced intriguing shapes which we would then try to interpret – rather like reading tea leaves at the bottom of a cup.

My father had married Hilda Loewe, and together they had emigrated to England in 1934 under the protection of a wealthy society lady and amateur singer, Mrs Molly Miller-Mundy, who financed her own concerts world-wide and wanted Hilda all to herself as an accompanist. Molly was a faded beauty with red hair. She had a good, if light, soprano voice and sang mainly Irish songs, having come to London from Ireland. She had appeared with the famous Gaiety Girls and was soon to marry Major Miller-Mundy, whose estate near Andover supplied cattle for the King's herd. Her high-society connections were also expected to help my father's career as a portrait painter. However, the decision to accept Molly's patronage was probably influenced by the rise of the Nazis in Germany and the atrocities committed against Jews under the protection of the Third Reich.

The decision to move to England proved crucial to my future. Although my father and his new wife initially lacked work permits, they were gradually able to establish themselves as self-supporting artists and in 1937 took out a 21-year lease on a house with a large studio in Elm Tree Road, St John's Wood, London, close to Lord's Cricket Ground and also close to the Abbey recording studios where 'Aunt Hilda' frequently accompanied famous singers. It was a good choice – the L-shaped road boasted many distinguished and well-to-do residents and became a millionaire's row after the war. As sitting tenants when the lease ran out in 1958, they were safe from eviction and continued to live there for a modest rent, in keeping with their relatively modest income.

A few weeks after the Anschluss I began to notice that my mother was making frequent morning visits to the British Embassy's consular section. Later, I realised that she was waiting for my visa to come through and that my father had given the necessary guarantees to enable me to join him in England. It did not occur to me then that my father had refused to give the same guarantees for my mother and that she had decided to make the sacrifice of parting with her son to ensure his safety.

I was still away in the country when the visa finally came through. Hurried arrangements were made for my departure. Somehow my grandmother had managed to raise the money for an air ticket. Flying was considered far safer than a journey by train, not just because of my tender age, but also because railway travellers were often turned back at the border.

I clearly remember the scene on the spectator's terrace of the small terminal building at Vienna's Aspern airfield, while my mother, grandmother and I were waiting for the flight to be called. At one point, my mother drew me aside and quickly put some notes into one of my pockets. Money was too tight for my grandmother to be allowed to see this, but a plain-clothed Gestapo man did!

It did not occur to me that I might be parting from my mother for good. Also, I cannot remember exactly what she told me about her own situation. I think she asked me to persuade my father to help her come to England. Looking back on that parting, I fear my mother must have been heart-broken at the unfeeling way I said good-bye.

The three engines of the Junker Ju52 Lufthansa plane were already spluttering when I walked to board with the 20 or so passengers. I felt under enormous pressure, the rotating propellers were urging me on – a need to get on board safely. I could not have heard the hurried steps behind me. Suddenly, someone in uniform grabbed me and marched me back to an office in the terminal. "What did your mother give you on the terrace?" they kept asking, unconvinced that it was only money. They let me go in the end, but not before they had confiscated the illegally carried currency and, as I found out, telephoned their colleagues in Frankfurt – the last stop before leaving Germany.

What must my mother and grandmother have felt when they saw me taken back to the terminal? And the relief to see me hurry back and get on the waiting plane!

So I set off on a seven-hour flight to London's Croydon Airport, with stop-overs at Salzburg, Munich, Frankfurt and Brussels. The Junker Ju52 with its three engines and corrugated aluminium wings never flew higher than 3,000 feet and in my frightened state and the constant turbulence, I was horribly sick all the way.

At Frankfurt Airport, before leaving the German air space, I had to strip and was subjected to a rigorous search. They even looked under my tongue because my speech was slurred from air sickness. The police must have had a tip-off from Vienna that I was a potential carrier of valuables. Jews allowed out of Germany had to leave all possessions behind.

When I finally arrived at Croydon Airport in a rather pitiful state on the 22nd September 1938, my father chose to greet me with these disapproving words: "Did you know there were Swastikas on the wings of your plane?" Had I shown him my passport, he would have been even more upset – the front cover displayed *Deutsches Reich* and a Swastika. Inside it was the precious visa allowing me to enter the United Kingdom. It had cost five shillings and sixpence and innumerable visits to the Vienna consulate by my mother.

What was interesting about my passport was the absence of a large encircled 'J'. Was I too young for this stigmatizing marker, or was it the fact that my mother had declared me as *konfessionslos* in my records?

Chapter IV
A New Life in England

I had arrived in England almost one year before the outbreak of the Second World War. It had to be a year of rapid adjustment.

My father and Aunt Hilda, who would eventually become my stepmother, wisely decided to send me to a boarding school, away from their busy lives and better placed to learn English quickly. They chose Quernmore School for Boys in Sundridge Park, Bromley, Kent. This school offered reduced rates for 'refugee' children – I seem to remember £22 instead of £36 per term – and I was soon joined there by paternal cousins Felix and his brother George, who had managed to emigrate from Czechoslovakia with their parents, Uncle Bruno and Aunt Frieda.

Aunt Hilda brought me to the school; I was not to see her for another six months. Soon after my arrival, I was interviewed by the head prefect, a burly lad who, I found out later, could weald a size 11 slipper with devastating effect if we, the smaller boys, failed to do his bidding. He asked if I could speak English and I weakly replied, "Fifty-fifty" – so cowed was I by his presence. I also found out later on that the headmaster's cane was infinitely less damaging than the slipper, as teachers exercised no control over the punishment meted out by prefects.

The school was obviously in financial difficulties and cut corners wherever possible. One consequence of this was that we were always hungry and had to top up with food sent or brought in from the parental home, or from local shops which meant a risky expedition over the school wall. Cousin Felix, two years my senior, often scaled the wall for more exiting adventures. He would creep into the dormitory late at night and he greatly impressed the rest of us with his daring.

We found a way of sharing our spoils. We had buttered bread and jam for tea and were allowed to ask for more buttered slices. The donor at each table would hand round his contribution – a tin of baked beans, salad cream or, a special favourite, Velveeta cheese. The small quantity thus allocated to each boy would then be stretched to the limit over as many slices as possible. The result was a never-ending queue at the kitchen hatch for more bread and butter, until one day a red-faced Mr Lightowler, the headmaster and owner, burst into the dining room in a rage, protesting that we had consumed 25 loaves and would only be allowed tinned fruit in future.

Breakfast was another time to supplement rations and indulge one's preferences, always providing one had something desirable to offer in exchange. I was lucky to receive chocolate marshmallows fairly regularly. These were in great demand from boys who did not like fishcakes, which I did.

When not being bartered, the popularity of the marshmallows priced them at no less than four pence each, enough to buy a ham sandwich at the bar of the sports club in Bromley to which we were taken once a week for a swim. The club was a type of venue entirely new to me, as was the seating in the coach that got us there; I had never experienced upholstered seating in a bus before, neither had I ever set foot in such smart and so very English club premises.

Other than the headmaster's son, the teachers seemed poorly qualified and poorly motivated. No doubt, their moral was low; the school was under threat of closure (it closed the following year) and goodness knows what they were paid! Luckily, my three years of secondary schooling in Vienna had advanced me academically beyond the standard of the other boys in my class, but there was the lack of English and I concentrated on catching up.

In fact, looking back, it is astonishing how fast a young brain can absorb knowledge. When Aunt Hilda came to collect me after a continuous six months at the school, she was quite amazed.

Apparently I never stopped chattering in English all the way to the St John's Wood home.

The house in Elm Tree Road with its old-world charm and secluded garden had been chosen by my father because of a large, separate studio building at the back. Here Emlyn Williams would come to be painted as Richard III, the Aeolian Quartet would rehearse and I would one day hold my wedding reception. The house itself was built over the foundations of a hunting lodge from the days when royalty hunted in the Wood. It had been recently renovated and was a poor example of building standards. Its fabric gradually deteriorated until at the time of my father's death in 1988, several rooms were no longer safe to enter.

Early in 1939 whilst at St John's Wood, my father gave me a letter from my mother. I had already heard from her a few times from Vienna, showing concern for me, describing her efforts to get out of Austria and urging me to persuade my father to help her. This was the first letter to come from outside Austria. She had finally managed to get out of the country with help and encouragement from her friend from student days, Käthe Caliò, and she eventually found shelter with her high up in the South Tirolean mountains, where Käthe was able to survive by teaching the children of local farmers.

My mother was destitute; this time her letter implored me to ask my father once more for help. I was well aware of my father's attitude towards his ex-wife's plight from previous occasions, but I plucked up courage and pleaded with him. The result was predictable: my father flew into an uncontrollable rage and told me never to broach the subject again. I did not. Perhaps it was cowardly of me, but what could I do and what would have changed his mind? I was thirteen and thoroughly intimidated, knowing no-one in what was still a strange country.

Would my father have helped if he had known what was to come? The honest answer has to be: I don't think so, because he knew better than most what was happening under the Nazis. He gave up portrait painting in 1938 to devote himself to producing political cartoons warning of the dangers of appeasement with Hitler's Germany. He frequently cited 'Mein Kampf' to make his point, because Hitler's plans were there in that book, written in prison in 1924, and they were becoming a reality. And already in 1938 he had drawn a concentration camp with a long line of Jews entering through the open jaws of a skull under the glare of searchlights and guarded by menacing armed storm troopers, a blood-red setting sun in the background.

After that letter from her, I wrote to my mother twice. I felt sure that we would soon be re-united. At that time, I did not foresee a prolonged war and the idea that Jews in Italy would eventually be rounded up and sent to the gas chambers did not even occur to me.

I did not receive any other letters from my mother, but I discovered after my father died that she had written two more, each time in greater desperation. Did my father withhold the letters to avoid further pleading from me? Was it an act of perverted kindness, not to put me under pressure? Was it Aunt Hilda who played Lady Macbeth in the whole tragedy? These questions can never be answered!

Later in life, when the enormity of the Nazi crimes and my mother's tragic fate had come to light, I would try to come to terms with my impotence in the face of my father's refusal to help the woman he must once have loved. I would even make excuses for him. He too could not have anticipated what would happen to her in Italy, and Hilda, his second wife, would surely have vetoed any move to bring my mother to England. Nevertheless, a strong feeling of guilt has remained with me all my life; a guilt that became almost unbearable on reading an Italian researcher's detailed account of how she had managed to survive until February 1944 and her terrifying final days at the hands of the Germans.

One day at the boarding school, I decided to try smoking. I had been impressed by the way the headmaster's son seemed to acquire considerable poise by smoking a pipe; knowing just when to light it, how to hold it and when to suck it for maximum effect. So I went to Woolworth's Threepenny and Sixpenny Stores, bought a sixpenny pipe and three penny's-worth of Players Digger's Shag and took these into the bushes at the bottom of the playing field. The effect of smoking a raw pipe with the strongest tobacco on sale was devastating; I could not even crawl back to the house when the bell for the early evening 'homework' class sounded.

The school may have been in decay, but there was much that was beneficial in the three terms I spent there. My English improved to the point where I was able to pass a grammar school entrance examination; I was able to enjoy organised sport for the first time even though I was usually the fall guy as wicket or goalkeeper, and I learned how to socialise with English boys.

Preparations were gathering momentum for a war that now seemed inevitable. By the time I left the boarding school after the summer term, sandbags were appearing everywhere, cast iron railings disappeared from park fences, people with gardens were busy installing Anderson shelters and the evacuation of children from London had begun. Munich and "peace in our time" was now just a reminder of the futility of appeasement, but perhaps the sham treaty Hitler had offered gave Britain more time to prepare.

Chapter V
The War Years

My father and Aunt Hilda decided that I too, should be sent into the country. Through some friends of theirs I was made to join a school in Finchley, which was to be evacuated to Biggleswade in Bedfordshire. So we foregathered at the school, gasmasks and identity tags hanging from our necks, to await transportation by bus and train to Biggleswade, a very peaceful and typically provincial town.

I had teamed up with a 16-year-old German boy and we were first billeted with a middle-aged and middle-class lady who treated us with great suspicion from the start. After only three days she decided she did not want 'enemy aliens' in her house and we were duly moved to a working-class family who, in contrast, treated us with great kindness and generosity. This was my first lesson in English class distinctions and it left a lasting impression in favour of working people.

On the morning of 3rd September, I was in the local park listening on a public address system to Neville Chamberlain declaring that we were at war with Germany from 11 o'clock. A few minutes later the air raid sirens sounded and we were all scanning the sky, waiting to be bombed and gassed. Nothing happened, of course, and the uneventful weeks that followed gave us all a false sense of security.

There were problems. The school from Finchley turned out to be a fairly orthodox Jewish institution and it only catered for boys up to fourteen. My friend and I were too old for lessons, but we were expected to act as elders at religious services. I wanted to conform and so I simulated prayer with much mumbling and bowing, trying very hard to do the right thing at the right time.

Most, if not all the children, must have come from homes with kosher kitchens and now found themselves in far-from-Jewish billets. I never found out whether they had a special dispensation from their Rabbi, justified by emergency circumstances, to eat food provided by Gentiles.

Our kind hosts consisted of father, mother and three grown-up bachelor sons. One was a baker, one a bus driver, the third I cannot remember. With three sons bringing home their earnings, the family was not poor and hearty Bedfordshire food, such as boiled beef, steak pies and steak and kidney puddings, was in plentiful supply, as were the splendid Bedford Brussels sprouts just coming on stream.

Although the sons, and especially the bus driver, took it in turn to take us out, a life of leisure can become boring after a few weeks. So when a local newsagent advertised for a young assistant, I applied and got the job at ten shillings a week. I proudly wrote to tell my father the 'good' news, only to be told to return to London immediately, my education had to continue.

By this time it was nearly Christmas and there were still no serious air attacks. Life was fairly normal in London during the day and I remember being taken to what I believe was called the London School of Cookery, to find out whether my childhood ambition to become a chef could be realised. Alas, the headmaster made me feel thoroughly rejected by saying that mine was the wrong background for taking up such a menial occupation. I was not from the working classes and would never fit in. I suppose his perception of a cook was a far cry from the exalted status of today's executive chef and I would probably never have made it to the top echelons of *haute cuisine*, given the kind of basic training the school would have provided.

Exactly how it came about I do not know. Not far from St John's Wood, on the corner of Marylebone Road and Lisson Grove, there was an old-established and esteemed establishment, the

St Marylebone Grammar School, which had been evacuated to Redruth in Cornwall. Aunt Hilda had arranged for me to take an entrance exam at its Marylebone Road premises. I was successful and joining this exceptional school was, I believe, to prove crucial in shaping my future.

I arrived in Redruth in the first days of 1940 and was first billeted with a family that obviously expected to make a profit from the seven shillings and sixpence a week they were paid for my board and lodgings. Apart from that, there were two sex-starved daughters in the house and the place was none-too-clean.

I was soon moved from there after discovering creepy-crawlies – not to mention the older daughter – in my bed. My next billet was with an accountant and his wife in a house on a terrace overlooking the town. They were kind people who looked after me as a contribution to the war effort. In some ways I tried to repay that kindness by helping to tidy the garden and doing other chores, and by pretending that I did not take sugar in tea, which helped to eek out the meagre rations. It was whilst staying there in 1941 that I received a notification from the Red Cross to advise me that my mother had been reported missing. It did not tell me anything new, but it came as a profound shock – the realisation that I had almost lost sight of her in pursuit of my new life. For the first time there was a feeling of guilt because I was safe and my mother was not.

When I arrived in Redruth, there were still no premises available to house the London school and we had to share the local county school with lessons only every second day. This gave us a lot of leisure time which was taken up constructively with various activities organised by the masters. A few months later we were able to occupy the Wesleyan Chapel in the High Street, which provided surprisingly suitable accommodation. Although we now had lessons five days a week, the extra-mural activities kept growing.

With the sea at Portreath only four miles away, a small carpenter's shop was opened for the production of surfboards. Surfing was good on this part of the Cornish north coast and some of us became quite expert after the inevitable failed attempts to jump with the waves at just the right time, only to get the edge of the board rammed into the stomach.

We would cycle over the hill to Portreath on some old bikes obtained from goodness knows where. On the way we would pass spaced-out tin filtering stations, operated without machinery or attention by little streams of water flowing downhill.

We also formed a school brass band in which I manned the bass drum, an orchestra for which I started to learn the flute and even an Airforce Cadet band in which I banged the bass drum on the march wearing a leather apron.

Our science master had a keen interest in classical music. He invited some of us to his billet every Tuesday night to listen to gramophone records. My lifelong love of classical music was kindled by such pieces as Liszt's Hungarian Dances, which I thought the *ne plus ultra* at the time.

All 'Burtons the Tailors' had an assembly room above the shop and the Redruth branch was no exception. It became our rehearsal room for brass band and orchestra and it was also where we embarked on a giant mural covering the whole of the long inside wall.

Most boys participated in these extra-curricular activities with great enthusiasm, so my efforts were absolutely nothing out of the ordinary except, perhaps, for my part in the 'Dig for Victory' campaign.

Near the centre of town was an empty one-acre field, the site of a future post office. This was allocated to the school and I was put in charge of it to organise vegetable culture. About twenty boys were given a small plot each and had to contribute to the cost of seed, which I purchased and distributed. The results were not outstanding, but enough vegetables were grown to invite Redruth residents to come and pick their own – certainly the first time they had come across PYO. As a sideline, I began to harvest the watercress in a bordering stream and persuaded the then Curb Café opposite Charing Cross station to buy it from me. It was sent to London by train overnight. They also bought some mushrooms from me, grown with great difficulty – a venture I soon abandoned.

Evenings when there was nothing on were either spent at the local cinema, which provided more than three hours entertainment for sixpence, or we would investigate doorways and shop entrances to see what soldiers from the nearby barracks were doing with 'easy' local girls who would grant favours without even extinguishing their cigarettes. The display of sex between strangers and without love rather shocked me at first but, at 15, I still had a lot to learn. I was much too reticent to pursue girls, but one took a fancy to me. Sadly, the still innocent affair came to an abrupt halt when, on a visit to the seaside, I discovered that the unfortunate girl had dark hairs on her chest.

I was desperately hard-up most of the time. My father and Hilda seemed to think that, for what was now ten and sixpence, my landlady should provide everything including toothpaste and shoe polish. I was conscious of the fact that billeting me was already an act of charity and that I should not cause my hosts further expense. Pleading for more pocket money produced little result, so the only alternative, other than stealing, was to take up gardening work in my spare time, which I actually enjoyed, with cups of tea and much encouragement from my customers. I remember buying a pair of trousers for ten shillings with some of the money I earned. They lost their shape almost as soon as I put them on.

One of my gardening customers was a school teacher and the daughter of a farmer near Camborne. She was living on her own and I found that I had to keep my distance. However, she provided me with the opportunity to work on her father's farm in my school holidays. The farmer also had a son and a second younger daughter and we all got on very well together.

The work was hard, especially the harvesting, as most tasks had to be done by hand. With double summer time and the westerly position of Cornwall, there was light until nearly midnight and we would be stooking or loading sheaves of corn until far into the night, kept going by a shuttle of mugs of tea brought by the girls. When we were loading, I was the one up on the horse-drawn wagon literally catching the sheaves with my bare hands. Bristling with thistles, they came flying at me from the pitch forks, so expertly handled by farmer and son that there was hardly time to arrange them correctly, their cut ends facing outwards.

One of the highlights of my stay was the food, especially the delicious fruit pies made by the farmer's wife and served topped with Cornish crusted cream. The loganberry pies were particularly memorable.

I clearly remember the large pot on the cooking range, in which stood a basin of cream skimmed off the top of the churns before they were collected. The milk from the Shorthorns was very rich; the high-yield, low-fat Friesians had not yet dominated milk production. The water in the pot was kept very hot or gently boiling for what seemed like a day and a half and the result was heaven for a hungry sixteen-year-old.

I was treated as one of the family and was expected to attend Sunday Service at a nearby church. Once again, I was obliged to mumble, not knowing when to get up or when to sit down or when to kneel and knowing none of the hymns, let alone the Lord's Prayer.

Then one day in July 1941, on my second holiday spent on the farm, a policeman walked up the drive and asked to see me. As an 'enemy alien' having reached the age of sixteen, I had to have a Registration Certificate issued by Camborne police and thereafter needed to report my movements to the nearest police station.

From the moment the farmer and his family saw the Swastika on my passport cover, the friendliness was gone and suspicion took its place. Was I a spy? No matter how carefully I tried to explain my situation as a victim of Nazi Germany, relations were never the same again. They must have felt betrayed. They took me for an ordinary English boy and I had deceived them.

Apart from the large number of soldiers stationed around Redruth, there was an air base close by. This made the area a very desirable military target for German planes using mainly anti-personnel bombs. They were bombs with a long probe and they exploded above ground, scattering shrapnel in all directions. The effect was often devastating. One of our masters actually witnessed his wife's decapitation by a large piece of shrapnel and there were numerous cases of severed limbs and other horrible injuries. Redruth was certainly not the safe place for evacuees it was meant to be!

Despite such danger, the King and Queen once came through the centre of Redruth in an open car, having visited an ammunitions factory in Camborne. They looked so very colourful to me as they briefly stopped to talk to our headmaster, Mr P A Wayne. The King was our patron and the school had acquired a reputation for providing a thoroughly good, all-round academic and moral education. This was no doubt largely due to our enlightened headmaster who also coped brilliantly with the problems created by wartime conditions. Even when he caned me in front of the whole school for being rude to the very first female teacher in the school's history, I felt no resentment. I had ridiculed the embattled 26-year-old Miss Walker and, being a senior boy, had to be made an example of.

I had been put into the fourth form when I arrived in Redruth in early March 1940 and still had a bit of catching up to do in written English before joining the fifth form in September that year. Meanwhile, my father was interned on the Isle of Man, in a clean sweep of all 'enemy aliens' regardless of where their loyalties lay. Unfortunately, the soldiers rounding up what were mostly Jewish refugees, treated everyone as an enemy and rifle buts were used all too often to urge their charges on.

Hilda was incensed by the detention of her Otto, the portrait painter now turned cartoonist, who had worked ceaselessly to expose

Hitler's real intentions when governments preferred to believe the dictator's assurances, and who was already supporting the war effort with fierce anti-Nazi propaganda before his internment. She worked ceaselessly to secure his release and paid three visits to the Isle of Man camp to talk to him across the wire fence.

Largely through her efforts, my father was not only released after six months but, on returning, was immediately asked to work for the then Ministry of Information. He was instructed under conditions of great secrecy, to produce five cartoon sketches each week, of which three would be selected by officials to be turned into finished artwork. His propaganda cartoons were used for leaflets dropped from the air and also published in various underground newspapers, notably in *La France Libre*, the paper of the Free French.

My father worked for the Ministry throughout the war, producing powerful images prophesying the defeat of Germany. His reward came in 1946 when he was invited to attend the Nuremberg Trials. 60 portraits of the accused and a full view of the dock are now in the Imperial War Museum.

It is now well-known that there was a remarkable convergence of talent amongst the Jewish refugees brought together in the internment camps. My father was one of the inmates who contributed to the flourishing cultural life of the camp by drawing many of his fellow internees and by giving lessons. Apart from that, he was responsible for cooking porridge and preparing breakfast for the sixty occupants of his hut.

As a result of my father's encounter with other artists in the internment camp, he had many refugee visitors to his studio in St John's Wood, some of whom rose to great heights in Britain's cultural life. It was also the beginning of a long friendship with the members of the Aeolian Quartet who were regularly invited to use the studio for rehearsals.

My last year at St Marylebone Grammar School started in September 1941. The Blitz on London was at its height and prompted me to write my first poem entitled, 'A Night in an Air Raid Shelter'. I sent it to father with the following pathetic and presumptuous preamble: "My dear Otto, there's a motto hidden somewhere in these lines, to remind you, that I asked you, to abandon London." My father would on no account leave his studio and Hilda's work when she was not travelling with ENSA, was in London. So they stayed put and spent each night in a nearby shelter under a block of flats, until the German raids stopped.

The third term in the Upper Fifth saw me completely unprepared for the General School Certificate examination that would end my school days. In something of a panic a couple of weeks before the exam, I swatted day and night and managed to pass, helped in oral French and German by a conversation in German with the examiner, who then did not bother with my rather poor French. I was not a good pupil; I was lazy and neglected the subjects that did not interest me.

Nevertheless, my marks were just good enough to give me exemption from matriculation – a wartime shortcut to ease entry into higher education. My father may have wanted me to continue with studies, but as an 'enemy alien' and seventeen-years-old, I was obliged to choose between the Pioneer Corps, the mines, farming or engineering.

Unfortunately, my enthusiasm for growing things made me choose to work on a farm. It turned out to be a bad choice because I was unlucky with the farm to which I was sent. This was a 60-acre mixed farm in Oxfordshire run by the farmer and his wife with no apparent assistance – at least not until I arrived on the scene. The couple treated me like a prisoner of war; I was made to work from four or five in the morning depending on the season, until quite late in the evening. My first daily job was to bring in the thirty or so cows for milking. Finding the cows in the dark on a misty morning and making sure that they entered the stables in the correct pecking order, was often a nightmare. If bovine seniority was not observed, there would be an almighty scuffle and all would scramble out again.

Out in the fields in the misty darkness, I learned to listen for a cough. The sound would lead me to the herd. Next, I had to find and persuade the head cow to get up and make for the stables. This would usually result in the rest of the herd following in the right order. But all too often, a young animal would barge into the stable ahead of an older one and we were back to square one!

Working on my own, it was important to see all the cows safely settled in their boxes, where they would usually wait to be chained up. But any upset would see them all out in the yard again.

Then came the morning's worst job: washing their underbellies and udders with cold and all too often, ice-cold water. This cruel exercise did nothing for hygiene, but it satisfied the regulations.

The main part of the milking was done by Alfa Laval machines after which the cows had to be 'stripped' by hand to squeeze out the last of the milk. This was done by repeatedly running thumb and index finger down each teat. The temptation was to lubricate the fingers with milk to speed things up – again hardly hygienic!

Quite often, I would amuse myself by squirting milk in the direction of the farm cat which promptly sat up to catch it. Once, in an unguarded moment, the cow I was stripping became irritated and put its muddy hind leg into my nearly full bucket. What was I to do? Upset the farmer or put it into the cooler in the hope that the contamination would not be noticed. My cowardly decision was to add the milk to the rest. A few weeks later, the farmer lost his license for the purest grade of milk and I had to accept the blame.

Working so early in the morning had its reward: a farmhouse breakfast served at around nine o'clock which, luckily, I was allowed to share. It would have turned people on rations green with envy. It was a copious meal, eaten with a voracious appetite, and it set one up to face the rest of the day's work.

After nearly twelve months, the period of hard labour came to an end when the kindly wife of a neighbouring farmer persuaded me that I did not have to put up with such harsh working conditions. Apparently she had been in touch with the authorities and had reported what she considered to be abuse. I checked with the local police and was allowed to go back to London and to choose another of the occupations open to me.

To my surprise, the labour exchange sent me to a Paddington firm which was contracted to fit blackout curtains to public buildings, such as schools and hospitals in London and the Home Counties. We used a standardised system and two of us were able, with practise, to fit a normal window in less than half an hour. Classified as war work, it was repetitive, but took us to ever-changing and often interesting venues.

Whenever we returned to the firm's premises, we would end the day with a visit to a pub near Sussex Gardens – an area noted for heavily made-up ladies walking small dogs, usually white poodles, at night. They often came into the pub, not to find customers, but for a rest and a chat. Invariably, they would tell you that the only reason they had joined 'the oldest profession', was to keep a son at university or that they had made the sacrifice for some other worthy cause. At the age of eighteen their stories, true or false, certainly broadened my outlook. I also enjoyed being among real working-class people in Paddington area, something that had not happened since I was first evacuated to Biggleswade.

Just before the firm's contract ended, we were working at a TB sanatorium in Milford, Surrey. It was the poor person's alternative to the expensive King Edward VII sanatorium at Midhurst. In spite of a large number of terminally ill patients, it was a cheerful, sunny, place. There was a spirit of defiance among the younger inmates, some of whom would abscond during the evening to spend time in the village pubs. I was greatly attracted to one of the patients, a very pretty young girl of around 20, and we spent quite a bit of time chatting. She was the picture of health and I thought she must be well on the way to recovery, until I was told that her rosy cheeks signalled the final stage of consumption.

The sanatorium was looking for a temporary laboratory assistant to help with a special investigation. I applied and got the job, which proved most interesting, if rather gory. The main task was to dissect and examine the lungs of patients who had died in order to establish the exact cause of death.

What the study showed was that not all the patients had died of TB. Some of them were ex-soldiers who had been gassed during World War I. Almost all of them had taken to chain smoking around the clock as a way of alleviating their tormenting symptoms. The cause of their death was a thick layer of tar which had stopped the absorption of oxygen and the removal of carbon dioxide through the *alveoli* on the lung surfaces.

This was before antibiotics came into general use and when the main treatments for TB were rest, a body-building diet and good fresh air, or surgery. If one of the lungs was badly affected and the other healthy, there were two types of surgical procedures. One was to cut a gap in the nerve controlling the lung to collapse it and give it a chance of recovery before the nerve grew together again. The size of the gap would determine the length of time the lung remained out of action.

The second procedure involved more drastic surgery and was used when a lung was considered beyond recovery. In this case it was permanently collapsed by removing a piece from each of the ten ribs on the side of the affected lung. Unfortunately, the remaining lung often became diseased as well and the outlook then became hopeless.

When the temporary job at the sanatorium ended, my choice among the occupations open to me was clear: it had to be engineering. I enrolled at the Government Training Centre in Acton and learned some of the basics of mechanical engineering. After about three months, when it became apparent that I was good with my hands, I was streamed into the toolmaking section of the Centre and given a six-month course which also involved learning how to use standard machine tools.

Whilst at the Training Centre I was embroiled in a curious adventure with Vera, a pretty, slightly tubby trainee, who was obviously a young virgin anxious to experience sex, and who had singled me out for that purpose. To achieve her aim, she went to extremes by telling me that she was pregnant and that her doctor had advised sexual intercourse as a means of terminating her unwanted pregnancy! Furthermore, she had befriended a middle-aged lady at the Centre, who offered the use of her vacated flat for this medically inspired exercise. I will admit to going along with this, but must spare the reader the embarrassing details of a disastrous encounter.

By this time it was 1944, I was nearly nineteen and had finished my training course. The war in Europe was being won, but there was still some way to go to final victory. Suddenly I had an overwhelming urge not to be left out. I went to a recruitment centre in Tottenham to enrol in the army. Instead of being found out as an 'enemy alien' who would have to join the pioneer corps, I was informed that toolmaking was a reserved occupation – they could not take me.

I reported back to the Government Training Centre and was allocated to a small engineering firm, Dawson & Co in Surbiton, Surrey, at a basic weekly wage of three pounds and ten shillings and a take-home pay of five pounds with overtime, plus an unspecified occasional bonus. That was not bad money for a lad still eighteen with no track record in toolmaking.

Dawson & Co was located in St Mary's Road off Victoria Street, Surbiton. The premises consisted of two corrugated iron sheds, joined together at right angles. Each shed had a round stove in the middle with a flue pipe going up through the roof. Without any insulation or other form of heating, it was a very cold place during the one winter I spent working there. But the atmosphere was warm and friendly – a real wartime spirit prevailed.

The friendly atmosphere was greatly helped by Jenny's Café across the road from the workshop. Each morning at about 10.30 we would send for chunky slices of fresh, yeasty bread, generously covered in delicious beef dripping with lots of heavy brown streaks full of meat flavour. This copious mid-morning snack, costing one penny would see us through till 1.00 pm, when several of us would march across for a main course, sweet and a cup of tea for just one shilling and fourpence! With meagre rations and only a gas ring to cook on, Jenny's became an indispensable part of my working week.

I say meagre rations, but in fact I did get a few extras from the lady assistants in Sainsbury's opposite the station. They must have felt a little motherly towards a young lad living on his own. There were usually some cracked eggs, off-cuts and un-rationed but scarce items saved for me, and they helped to make home-cooked meals more varied and plentiful.

The primitive accommodation at Dawson & Co betrayed the precise nature of the work, much of it connected with making accurate fixtures for producing ammunitions. I was the new boy among eleven other employees and I had to learn fast. One section of the workshop was making filler gauges for small arms ammunition. The first operation on a grinding machine was to cut a slot into the hardened body of the gauge and the second and final operation was to precision-grind a central pin which would control the amount of gunpowder injected into the cartridge. I made these jobs my own and was able gradually to step up production. The extra output contributed to a bonus payment and helped me to integrate with the small and diverse engineering community of which I was now part.

I really needed the money. At a rent of 30 shillings a week I had found a bed-sit with a gas fire and gas ring in Browns Road. I also had to feed and clothe myself. All of this would have been managable; the problem was the cost of any kind of social life.

Buying the odd pint during a game of snooker in the pub on the corner did not cause any difficulty; it was when I decided to attend the Carl Bryant School of Dancing on the corner of Victoria Street and Surbiton Station forecourt that cash flow problems really began. Whilst attending the classes was affordable, the cost of buying drinks for a girl during the interval was not. However, it was the price one had to pay to have any chance of walking her home and getting a good-night kiss.

There were no girls to befriend at Dawson's. The only young and attractive woman in the workshop was having an affair with Michael, a suave Rumanian in charge of a large Wilson lathe. She operated a small Southbend lathe opposite him. Her husband was away in the war, and she was always on guard in case we should find out about her transgression.

An interesting character among us was an older man who had been a sergeant in WWI and, he claimed, footman to the Prince of Wales for a time. He had a lot to tell us about the conditions the soldiers had to suffer in that terrible war and made us realise how lucky we were to be able to lead comparatively normal lives in relative safety. Apart from some interesting anecdotes, he told us he was sure that the heir to the throne had suffered a serious riding accident and that it had left him impotent. Having read the Prince's wartime letters to Mrs Freda Dudley Ward, I rather doubt the truth of that little story.

One evening at Carl Bryant's, I spotted a new arrival in the company of a regular girl. She was stunning, quite tall and shapely, with gorgeous auburn hair and an attractive face that radiated a sunny smile. To me she was a great prize, worth making sacrifices for. And so it was that I found myself paying three-and-sixpence a time for the cherry brandies she liked, and going broke by the end of the week.

Edna (Viki) Fawcett lived with her mother at 49 Portsmouth Road in a flat overlooking the Thames. Having escorted her home a few times and received appropriate but oh-so-proper good-night rewards at the door, I felt encouraged to suggest that we take the school's courses together as dancing partners. By the time we had passed bronze, silver, gold and gold cross exams, we were deeply in love. We stayed partners-in-life, and in January 1948 embarked on a marriage that was to last until 2006, when Viki died of a brain tumour.

The Fawcett family was resident in Liverpool, where Viki's great great-grandfather had opened a factory with a man called Bley, making a new and more nutritious ship's biscuit based on pea flour. Fawcett biscuits were not only an essential and preferred item on long voyages before refrigeration and freezing came into general use, but they had also become quite fashionable in spite of their peas-pudding flavour and tooth-breaking texture. They were still available in the sixties from such iconic establishments as Fortnum & Mason of Piccadilly!

Inevitably, demand for the biscuits ceased, the factory closed and the modest family fortune was soon dissipated. Edward Fawcett was considerably older than Viki's mother and this may have contributed to her parent's decision to divorce when she was about twelve. She had lived mostly in Sefton Park, Liverpool, until then and was now to move to Greater London with her mother, who wanted to be nearer to her family, Viki's grandparents and her uncle.

The war was still very much in evidence in the late spring of 1944. Large-scale bombing raids had stopped; instead a new type of plane appeared, first during the night. I was in the Home Guard and on air raid duty when searchlights picked out an aircraft and the anti-aircraft guns immediately went into action. A few moments later there was a big explosion on the ground and we were congratulating ourselves that another 'jerry' had been shot down. Of course, it was a 'doodlebug', a V1 flying bomb that was meant to explode on the ground. These 'secret weapons' were either activated to dive down when they had reached their intended destination, or their trajectory was controlled by the amount of fuel they carried. Shot down over London, they did exactly what they were intended for.

The V1 assault intensified for a time; the flying bombs were coming over in formation. Barrage balloons did not seem effective, but fighter pilots who went out to meet them had learned to fly alongside and to tip their wings, diverting them to crash in less populated areas.

The damage caused by these bombs could be quite horrific. They had to be relatively light and carried a massive amount of explosive in a thin shell. Buildings hit would first blow up and then implode, leaving the victims trapped under the rubble or thrown on top of it. One particularly bad night, a bomb came down in the area where Viki and her mother lived. I jumped on my bike and raced down the hill towards the Portsmouth Road. It was the house next-but-one, and there was my girl, knee-deep in rubble on what had been the roof, her legs covered in blood, frantically trying to release a man trapped under the debris. It was a sight that bonded me with her and instinctively made me a truly loyal friend for the rest of her life.

Sometimes the flying bombs would destroy one half of a building, leaving the other half practically undamaged. From a distance the undamaged part would look like a doll's house, a half of every room on every floor remaining intact. Sadly, there were a lot of casualties because most people no longer went into shelters; the raids were too random and the warnings were unreliable.

The V1s were followed by the V2 rockets, the even-more-secret weapon with which Hitler hoped to bring Britain to its knees. I think the first one fell by the side of Selfridges producing a huge crater and destroying an exhibition of my father's cartoons on the top floor. No one knew what had caused the explosion. It was officially explained as an exploding gas main, but it was not long before the truth was known. What was particularly frightening about these missiles was that they could not be heard until they exploded.

Needless to say, the launch pads for V1 and V2 weapons came in for intensive attacks by the allies, but it was not always easy to locate them. They were mostly mobile and could be moved at very short notice. Fortunately, the advancing armies were soon to catch up with all the sites and stop any further attacks.

By the end of 1944, the military map of Europe had changed completely. Italy had already officially surrendered in September 1943 and German troops had moved in to join Fascist divisions fighting a rearguard action. On 6th June, the allies landed on the Normandy beaches, by August Paris was liberated and by December, the Rhine was reached. Meanwhile the Russians had driven the German armies out of their country, fought their way across Poland and were about to discover the horrors of Auschwitz.

I was so unthinking and so absorbed with my own life, it simply did not dawn on me that a German-occupied, Northern Italy meant that my mother's life was at risk. It took quite a time after the war before I knew with certainty that she could not have survived and many more years had to pass before the whole tragic story came to light.

In January 1945 Marshall Zhukov's men of the Red Army reached Auschwitz. They entered a death factory, where Jews from all over Europe were sent to be slaughtered or worked to death. Apart from mounds of skeletal corpses, the soldiers found about 5,000 prisoners still alive, but near death from starvation and disease. The images of the camp sent shockwaves around the world.

By March, the Russians were fighting in Berlin and Allied armies had crossed the Rhine. There were still some obstacles to victory in Europe, but now there could be no doubt that the war was won and that it had to be total and final surrender.

We did not have to wait very much longer. Germany formally surrendered unconditionally on 7th May 1945. The war was over and the time had come to count the cost.

Chapter V
Post-War Aspirations

Dawson & Co closed its doors well before the last shot was fired, leaving me out of a job. What next? My latest ambition was to become a market gardener, but I decide to stick with what I knew. I joined J H Farmer and Son, an engineering company next to the Town Hall in Kingston-upon-Thames, which was advertising for a toolmaker at quite an attractive wage.

The problem in those immediate post-war years was not demand, rather it was supply. Most materials needed for consumer goods were incredibly scarce or had been discontinued. Luckily, Farmer & Son had a large Government contract for making fighter aircraft propeller extractors, which had not been cancelled. The firm needed someone with toolmaking experience who could perform the precision finishing operations and take charge of a small production team. This was an opportunity to improve efficiency and increase output - a challenge I accepted with relish. The fact that I was able to almost double production was due largely to previous poor performance of the unit, but it nevertheless helped to boost my confidence as a budding engineer manager.

I moved from Browns Road in Surbiton into a small and simple boarding house in Fairfield, Kingston. It was owned by a Mrs Purfoy, who had a young, troublesome son, but no husband. The first thing I noticed about her was that the lower part of her face and some of her neck bore scars of severe burns. Later, I could not avoid the thought that this disfiguring injury might have been due to her husband's last cruel act before leaving her.

Mrs Purfoy fed her boarders well regardless of rationing. The breakfasts were often overpowered by the smell of kippers, the preferred dish of a Mr Ruskin, who nevertheless invariably complained about the bones. Derek Ruskin was a bank manager. Although he was renting separate rooms and came to breakfast alone, he was in fact 'living in sin' with a rather corpulent youngish lady called Doris. This had to be a well-kept secret to avoid any problems with his job at the bank.

Coming back from work, often quite late, I would look into the kitchen to see a well-filled plate of food sitting on top of a saucepan of boiling water. It would be covered by an inverted plate. This was my dinner; it was good basic grub, it was hot, and there was plenty of it.

On May 13, Winston Churchill announced to jubilant crowds in London that the war in Europe would end at midnight. Viki and I joined the night-long celebrations. There was much euphoria but, inevitably, it was short-lived. True, Germany was on its knees and the rest of Europe liberated, most of the Nazi hierarchy dead or captured, Mussolini lynched by his own people and the concentration camps freed. But in 'victorious' Britain, there was extreme austerity for years to come, an economy held back by a huge debt burden; and there was the gradual coming-to-terms with the scale of the disaster that Hitler had unleashed on Europe.

Japan still had to be defeated, but when atom bombs exploded over Hiroshima and Nagasaki on the 9th August, it took Japan only four days to surrender unconditionally. The secret weapon Hitler had hoped to use had dramatically defeated his cruel ally of the Berlin-Tokyo Axis. Once more, Britain celebrated. It was now all over.

The news of the atomic bombs on Japan came as Viki and I were returning from a cycle tour on my newly acquired, second-hand, Claude Butler tandem. We had cycled as far as Bristol and were coasting down the hill into Henley-on-Thames, when we spotted the Evening News placard: 'Atom bombs destroy Hiroshima and Nagasaki'. It was a great shock; the realization that humanity had created a weapon so powerful that it left a powerful enemy no choice but to surrender.

This particular cycle tour was also notable for the time we had to spend finding food. In Salisbury, on the way west, we finally tracked down a fish and chip shop that was actually open. Although not rationed during or after the war, the ingredients had to be fried in a white fat issued by the Government, which gave a decidedly 'candle-grease' flavour that increased each time the fat was re-heated. Needless to say, we were hungry enough not to notice as we picked our generously salted and vinegared fish and chips out of the newspaper wrapping.

That evening we got only as far as Wilton. A couple of large glasses of local cider whilst listening to farmers talking about "them rats" and their skill in catching them by their tails, had finished us off. We tried to cycle on, but only wobbled for a few yards before giving up and spending the night in an adjoining field. The problem of feeding ourselves was even worse in Bristol. We had arrived on a Sunday afternoon and everywhere was shut. When we did eventually find one open snack bar, all it could offer was a gassy, strawberry-flavoured drink. That evening, our stomachs empty, we consoled ourselves with a visit to a cinema. I can still hear Donald O'Connor singing: "You can't brush off a Russian, a Russian won't take brushin'!"

In one respect we were all lucky. Meals in restaurants were not rationed, except by price, and the only restriction was that fish and meat could not be served as part of the same meal. Even fashionable and expensive restaurants were not allowed to charge more than five shillings. Of course, there was a way around the price limit: the cost of drinks. Whenever we could afford it, Viki and I went to the Queen's Brasserie just off Leicester Square. It was a pleasant basement restaurant where we could dance to the music of Java and his Band; enjoy a good meal and a bottle of Hock for 30 shillings – the wine making up two thirds of the bill.

In view of the scarcity of food, some restaurants became quite creative. Chicken was often rabbit soaked in salted water to take away the gamey flavour, horsemeat would stand in for beef and whale meat appeared on menus for a time. I tried a whale dish once, but the pungent oiliness made me feel ill. On the other hand, I liked British Restaurants, where standardized, but well-prepared food was served. I particularly enjoyed Woolton Pie, vegetarian and the brainchild of Lord Woolton, the Food Minister.

The end of hostilities should have been the time for me to think of my mother, to start making enquiries and to keep hoping that she was safe. Writing this, I cannot remember my thoughts then. What I do know is that whilst I could have found out very little about her fate at that stage, I did not really try. I suppose I feared the worst, felt guilty and preferred to wait to hear.

I did not have to wait very long. The first indication that my mother could not have survived, came in January 1946 in a letter from Käthe Caliò, the friend who had sheltered her after her escape from Vienna. Käthe had been given my address by Uncle Richard, the lawyer who acted for mother in the divorce proceedings and who was still living in London before resuming his practice in Vienna. It was an emotional letter and the result of information she had received from an organisation based in Milan called the 'Jewish Committee'. Its records showed that Eva Haas-Flatter was arrested by the Germans towards the end of December 1943, imprisoned in Trento for nearly two months, taken to Fossili on the 15th February 1944 and sent to Auschwitz on the 21st.

Käthe's letter, which I have included in part II, is full of soul-searching and self-reproach. It is clear from this and subsequent letters that she was not only burdened by profound grief at the loss of a close and highly valued friend, but also by guilt for not having acted to prevent my mother's arrest – for not hiding her or asking a friend to do so.

At around this time I also began to hear from my maternal uncle, Benno. He had returned to Vienna and was re-united with my Aunt Mimi. Sadly, I learnt that my cousin Ditta had died of scarlet fever. Her younger sister Gerda, now grown-up, was working in one of the shoe shops restored to Herr Bitmann, the man my aunt had hidden throughout the war. Apart from personal news, these letters contained legal information, the detail of which I could not grasp, but it was clear that there were considerable legal obstacles to overcome before the family's property could be restored and might provide me with any financial benefit.

When the contract for propeller extractors finally ended at Farmer & Son, I was asked to make tools for saucepans, saucepan lids and egg poachers for a customer who had obviously managed to obtain some aluminium sheet. The new job was a bit of an anti-climax and made me weigh up my chances of starting my own toolmaking firm. My father had mentioned more than once that many Jewish industrialists fleeing the Nazis had been able to re-establish their factories in deprived areas of South Wales with financial help from the Government. Many of them were clustered in and around the Treforest Trading Estate, an industrial park north of Cardiff, quite close to Pontypridd and the meeting of the Rhondda Valleys at Porth. I would be sure, said my father, to get plenty of work from these firms. When asked, he agreed to lend me £500 which I undertook to pay back within two years. My father also produced an elderly and very Jewish businessman who owned a store near Watford filled with redundant machine tools, which he had promised to let me buy any I needed at 'Metzia' prices.

Working with me on tools for pots and pans was Frank Blowers, a skilled turner (lathe operator), recently divorced and keen to join me as a junior partner. So we set off together to take a look at the 'bargains' offered by my father's friend.

Most machines were old and worn and not that cheap either, but we soon discovered when we looked at better quality equipment, that my £500 would not have gone far enough. We decided we would have to take machines in need of reconditioning – something we were able to do, but it was an extra job that would delay much-needed earnings.

Viki's mother, Hilda Fawcett, died of cancer aged 47 just before I set off alone to South Wales in the notorious winter of 1946/7. I went there to find an affordable factory building, and suitable lodgings for two, in the deprived Rhondda Valleys. Losing what had been more like a sister and best friend was a cruel blow and left Viki on her own in the Portsmouth Road flat. I suggested she moved into my room in Fairfield, confident that I would no longer need it. Viki, who was an apprentice dispenser in Boots at the time, settled in well with Mrs Purfoy and stayed there until we married in January 1948.

I arrived in Cardiff at the height of the freeze-up. It was to be my base for the next few weeks whilst exploring the area around Pontypridd and Porth.

My limited budget did not permit staying at a hotel, so I looked for and found a simple room in a quiet part of town. On entering the room I was met by an icy blast and saw that there was a gas fire but no connection to the gas tap. Far from being an oversight, the missing rubber tube was only handed over by the landlady for a charge of one shilling, to be fed into the communal gas meter.

My journeys by train and bus were fraught with delays due to the severe weather. The further north I ventured, the more difficult travel became. Apart from snow and ice, there were many broken-down vehicles and, in the valleys, hundreds of dead sheep were lying by the roadside. They had come down from the hills in a desperate and vain search for food. At that time, many miners owned sheep. They branded them with their mark and then left them to roam freely on the hills. In that harsh winter of 1946/7, there was no way of saving these animals from starvation.

The contacts I had been given could not help with the 'affordable' premises I was looking for, but in Marcantonio's Café in Porth, the elderly owner pointed me in the right direction. Up the hill overlooking the town was Tynycymmer Hall – a grand-sounding name for a rather disreputable-looking place, more like a large stable with a loft. But it did have a flat, solid concrete floor and it was cheap. Trevor, who owned it, ran a pig farm at the back of the building, and we eventually had to learn to tolerate the revolting smell that invariably drifted our way; not so much from the pigs, but from the putrescent rubbish he boiled up for them.

After striking a bargain with Trevor, I had to look for nearby lodgings for myself and my new partner, Frank. Once again local knowledge came to the rescue. The first village up the Ferndale Valley was Ynyshir and a Mrs Cove resided on the main road running through it. She was well-established in the community as a shopkeeper selling wallpaper, and also for the hot faggots and peas she sold every Friday evening. I never found out how this combination of wares came about, but the shop was obviously a meeting place. Someone must have told someone that Mrs Cove was looking for lodgers to supplement her income. At 30 shillings each for full board seven days a week including our washing, this was another bargain I had to seal.

But was it such a tremendous bargain after all? Mrs Cove had been through the Great Depression. She was the only survivor of seven sisters; the other six had all died of consumption due to malnutrition. One had to remember her background and forgive the mean streak in her character. We even forgave her the Marmite sandwiches which turned up in our lunch pack with monotonous regularity month after month.

Mrs Cove would even use water with extraordinary care. On one occasion the gulley in the little courtyard at the rear of the house had become blocked and I was asked to investigate. Digging deep into the drain, I found the culprit. It was a pair of underpants belonging to me, but it was some time before I could work out how they got there. Apparently, the good lady was in the habit of washing our underwear in a little soapy water in the bathroom basin and then holding it in the lavatory pan whilst pulling the chain. My underpants had clearly got away!

On another occasion, we had roast pheasant over the weekend. It had been shot locally and bartered for Friday's faggots and peas. Some of it remained on the table after Sunday lunch, but not for long. When the house cat ran off with it, its owner sprang into action and followed in hot pursuit. The cat must have dropped its prize in fright, because a few moments later, a breathless Mrs Cove returned, wiping what was left of the bird with her apron. There was no escape; we had to have it for supper the following day!

Porth was then a modest town. Surrounded by hills, it was the gateway to the two Rhondda Valleys, with a busy main road carrying traffic from the south before dividing towards Treorchy and Ferndale. Next to Tynycymmer Hall was a small estate where a Mrs Evans, widow of the Evans in Thomas & Evans of 'Corona' drink fame resided in an imposing mansion. She had a reputation for meanness. In all probability she had been through the same hard school as my new landlady. Apparently, she never went out except when there was a cheap coach trip to Bari or Penarth, when she would sit on a seafront bench with her fellow passengers and eat fish and chips out of newspaper. It was even said that when Mrs Evans was given a spare turkey for the festive season, she put it in her fridge – yes fridge – to keep for the following Christmas!

Thomas & Evans had become a very large undertaking through the nationwide success of the 'Corona' drinks, but they also had a chain of grocery stores in South Wales. I soon discovered at their Porth branch and also in other food shops that the Welsh did not bother too much with rationing. This was a great comfort to Frank and me. We were working hard and for very long hours and we needed to supplement Mrs Cove's meals without being able to use our ration books which she held.

The family of a Swiss embroidery manufacturer, who had established a thriving business on the Treforest Trading Estate, occasionally provided me with a welcome distraction from the monotony of life in the Rhondda.

Josef Wlach had managed to bring his massive embroidery looms over from his factory in Brno, Moravia, ahead of the German invasion of Czechoslovakia. It was a remarkable feat, involving weeks of heavy assembly work, helped only by my cousin, Ernst, who was to marry Ilse, the elder daughter.

Depending on the size of the article, each of these looms could produce as many as 24 embroideries simultaneously, the row of needles being controlled by an operator using a pantograph. This device worked from a large pattern transposing, one by one, the magnified movement of the pantograph cursor into the fine spacing of the actual stitches. Years later, these manually operated machines would be replaced by computer controlled automatic looms.

Ernst Graumann was 17-years-old when he came to England from Prague. He was the son of my father's younger sister Klara and her husband Anton, a bespoke shoemaker. Ernst's parents had sent him to safety before the genocide of Jews in occupied Czechoslovakia claimed their lives.

The Wlachs had long been friends with the Flatters and both families were keen to have me marry Ilse's younger sister, Trude. Luckily, young Trude did not display any great enthusiasm for a romantic liaison, and I was able to continue to enjoy the family's hospitality without any ill-feelings.

I had registered the new company as Precision Tools (Glamorgan) Ltd. Once the machines were installed in Tynycymmer Hall and we had done all we could to improve their condition, it was time to find work. Demand for production tools was quite strong, but we soon found that about half the jobs for which we were asked to quote were beyond the capability of our out-of date machinery and, sometimes, beyond our skills. We managed to keep our heads above water for several months, but it was clear that there was no real future without a substantial injection of money for modern equipment.

At this point, my Uncle Bruno came to the rescue, not with money, but with a suggestion. He was my father's older brother (also not on speaking terms), and the father of my cousin Felix and his younger brother, George, who had been fellow pupils at Quernmore School in Bromley. Uncle Bruno and his wife Frieda, together with their two sons, had managed to come to England in 1938 from Brno in Moravia, and had established themselves in the haberdashery business. Aunt Frieda had organised a fleet of home workers who were paid so much per gross to paint buttons, broaches, bracelets and similar items. Whilst my aunt would sit in their little shop in Paddington, spending most of her time finding fault with the home workers' efforts, my uncle would be transacting business as wholesaler. Dealing with the haberdashery manufacturers populating the Birmingham area, he had discovered an unsatisfied demand for leather buttons and enquired whether I would be interested in producing these, using local people working from home.

Leather buttons worn on trench and sports coats are traditionally made from a long strip of malleable leather thonged into button shape and compressed under heavy pressure to form the finished button, which would then be coated with tinted shellac or pigmented leather paint. Producing a gross of unfinished buttons is very hard work and requires a great deal of skill and energy if it were not to take an inordinate amount of time. I could not see us training home workers to produce these thongs economically within a reasonable time frame, so I set about trying to find ways of producing the button mechanically, albeit in the form of a look-alike.

After several weeks of experimentation, I found a way of producing a button made from a petal-shaped blank piece of leather with a castellated metal crown in the centre. This clamped the four petals in a dome shape when the assembly was placed in a mould and compressed.

The buttons were required in six basic sizes and we had to make tools for them all, so that professional sample cards could be made and submitted for approval by my uncle's customers. Happily, the result of all that speculative work was a flood of orders. The button was patented and over the coming years literally millions left our little factory, boxed by the gross and sent to clothing manufacturers at home and abroad. Our toolmaking was now confined to refining and renewing our own production tools.

In spite of a steady order intake, cash flow – that wonderful synonym for a lack of cash – remained a problem. We had to find weekly wages for about 30 employees and our overheads had increased substantially. Luckily, Viki had by then joined us as company secretary and also as my wife. She was very good at persuading the manager of the Porth branch of the Midland Bank to grant us an overdraft until my uncle's anxiously awaited cheque arrived.

Viki and I were married on 16th January 1948; not the most auspicious time of the year and certainly not the best time to go to Llandrindod Wells for a honeymoon. The weather was atrocious; we went for walks in the rain and on one miserable occasion, got completely lost. I finished up feeling thoroughly ashamed of myself. With so little money to spend, we would have been far better off staying at home. Except that we had, as yet, no place to call our own.

I really was hard up; I had to have a pair of trousers dyed to match one of the two jackets I possessed, so that I could wear a 'dark suit' at my wedding. What turned the big day almost into a farce was that, working in Wales the previous day, I got six tiny metal chips stuck on the pupil of my left eye. I had stupidly used a grinding machine without wearing goggles. This meant a morning visit to the famous Surbiton Eye Hospital where, after the metal was removed, the nurses not only put an eye patch over my anesthetized eye, they wrapped me in bandages reaching right down across my chest. The fact that I was to be married later the same day caused great amusement, but also a warning to keep the dressings on. Of course, the bandages came off almost as soon as I left the hospital and by the evening, watching 'Oklahoma' in a smoky Drury Lane auditorium, the eye was almost unbearably sore.

The party which followed our Registry Office wedding took place in my father's studio. Thanks to Trevor of Tynycymmer Hall, food was plentiful. He not only supplied a leg of pork, he also got hold of a large salmon for me, goodness knows where from. The studio had a Bösendorfer grand piano in it and Hilda provided music for singing and dancing. There were probably thirty guests. Most of them brought presents; some met a real need and were greatly appreciated.

I left Mrs Cove and Ynyshir to join Viki in our first lodgings together, in Pontypridd on the road to Tonyrefail. It was not a happy place. Our landlady oozed frustration. It was clear she felt that she had married beneath her station. Her eyes had a most disconcerting nervous twitch. I do not remember any conversation with her except when she had a complaint. Her husband was a mousy little man who did not speak to us at all. On our first morning she chided Viki: "Your husband dropped his shoes on the floor last night." The most troubling of these complaints was about the number of times we had walked through their rear living room to get to the shared kitchen. There was no other way we could have arrived inside the house and so, to keep the peace, we used our French doors to the courtyard and from there, entered the kitchen through the rear door. Not very nice, especially when it was raining, but we were young, easily intimidated, felt very uncomfortable and decided to move out as soon as possible.

Our next lodgings – this time with half-board – were in Tonyrefail with a young family; a miner, his wife and their baby daughter. It meant a fairly long and very crowded bus journey. On these journeys I noticed that the conductor would not even try to work his way through the bus to collect fares. Instead, at each stop he would simply stand by the door and collect whatever he was given without issuing any tickets. It was a silent conspiracy, the passengers only paid about half the fare and most of the money undoubtedly went into the pockets of conductor and his driver. How the bus company ever made a profit, I never understood.

Mr and Mrs Williams were friendly, jolly people, but as the months passed it became clear that our consistently late arrival for supper was causing problems. We had to eat alone and were served spam and chips almost every evening. Eventually, the situation had to be confronted and we had to look elsewhere for accommodation.

At this time, Viki decided to give up her job in my firm. As an apprenticed dispenser, she was yearning to get back into a pharmacy. She left by amicable, mutual agreement and re-joined Boots the Chemists at its branch in Pontypridd. It was a good move. It brought in some much-needed extra money and because the branch manager and his wife took pity on us, we spent the remainder of Viki's stay in South Wales in their comfortable house and in very pleasant company.

Viki's place as company secretary was filled by Doreen, an intelligent and hard-working local girl who was in charge of our female workers and had become my partner Frank's girlfriend. The only real downside of this reshuffle was a strange reluctance by the Midland Bank manager to continue with the still necessary overdraft facility for paying the wages. Instead, I had to lean on my uncle for earlier payment.

It was not long before it became clear that Viki did not want to spend the rest of her life in South Wales and, as I had similar feelings, we decided that she should go back to London and that I would join her every second weekend until such time as I could profitably sell the business. She joined Boots in East Sheen, an area between Putney and Richmond-on-Thames, and found rooms in a semi-detached house owned by a Mrs Milroy, in Burdenshott Avenue, off the Richmond Road.

Now on my own, I decided not to stay with the Boots manager and his wife and instead found lodgings in Wattstown, a little further up the Rhondda Valley than Ynyshir, but still a lot closer to the factory than Pontypridd. My landlady was a Mrs White, the elderly wife of a miner who had died some years earlier. She was a very kind, unadventurous lady, who spent a large part of the day in the kitchen in front of the open hearth of her cooking range, her knees far too close to the burning coals. The fire was a comfort she could easily afford; as a miner's widow she was entitled to free coal. A welcoming pot of tea was always brewing on the range and local ladies would pop in for a bit of gossip whilst enjoying a cup of tea and the warmth of the fire.

Mrs White suffered from severe trigeminal neuralgia in the face and was sometimes driven to tears by the pain. Periodic injections helped, but sometimes lasted for only a few weeks. She bore this burden with great patience, never complaining. I got to like her for her undemanding nature and her stoicism in the face of considerable suffering. A few years later, when Viki and I had settled in London, we invited her to spend a couple of weeks with us. We made sure she had the time of her life with shows, sightseeing and excursions into the countryside. I can still see her sitting on the grass outside the Inn on the Green in Ockley, Surrey, unable to get up after two glasses of the local redcurrant wine!

It was now 1951 which was marked by two events, the first being the acquisition of a 1935 Austin 10, and the second, a visit to Vienna – our first holiday abroad – triggered by the prospect of money from my 'inheritance'.

New cars were extremely scarce and I could not have afforded one anyway. The Austin 10 was a solid car which had a sloping rear housing a tiny boot, a windscreen that opened manually and was fitted with manually operated wipers; indicator arms that often stuck; just one rear light; and brakes that became highly unpredictable when applied with force. The painfully sluggish 4-speed gearbox only had one synchromesh gear – first was a crash gear and second needed double declutching.

I used this car to travel between South Wales and London, often reaching the dizzy speed of 70mph. As a novice driver who had only just passed the driving test in a rented Ford Anglia, I suspect my life was at a greater risk during those hair-raising journeys, then at any time during WWII!

My destination was a house in Burdenshot Avenue, off Upper Richmond Road, owned by a Mrs Milroy. Viki had found quite spacious lodgings there and had once again joined Boots; this time in the East Sheen Branch of the Company.

Mrs Milroy was a heavily painted lady in her late sixties. Everything about her was theatrical, and we felt that we had to take much of what she said with a large pinch of salt. Her frequent complaints included problems with her heart, which we dismissed as part of 'the performance'. We were wrong! One day, about 18 months after we had moved in, Viki came home from work to find her lying on the kitchen floor. She had succumbed to a heart attack and it was not long before her son arrived, anxious to get rid of the lodgers.

What I remember most about this episode, was Viki's utter fascination with Mrs Milroy's mother, who was, it seemed, an even more theatrical lady in her early nineties and very much alive as the mistress of a wealthy admirer. He had established her many years ago in an apartment near Harrods in Knightsbridge (complete with step-in marble bath), where she still exercised her feline powers over him. I often wondered whether Viki's fascination with the old lady's exalted state was the thought that there was hope, even in old age!

Benno, my maternal uncle and black sheep of the family, had returned to Vienna soon after the end of the war and was accepted back by my Aunt Mimi and her now grown-up daughter, Gerda. Other than moving to another flat, my aunt had remained in the apartment block owned by my grandparents before the Anschluss in 1938. It was confiscated by the Nazis, and with both my grandparents dead (my grandfather had died in 1936 and my grandmother had perished in Belsen), the property was to be given back to the surviving family.

The private house in which I was brought up and which later served as an SS headquarters, had been taken over by a building society in rather dubious circumstances. The proceeds from its eventual sale (once our ownership had been restored) were to prove immensely useful to Viki and myself in getting established in London once again.

My one-third share of the apartment block on the other side of the garden was of little financial benefit (I later sold it for a nominal amount to my cousin Gerda). State-controlled rents from the apartments were hardly adequate to meet repair and maintenance costs for many years to come. It was not until the eighties and the end of the socialist government under Bruno Kreisky, that the owners could derive any revenue benefit from their property. Interestingly, Kreisky had the distinction of being the first Jewish Chancellor of Austria and also its oldest. Previously Foreign Minister, he became Chancellor from 1970 to 1983. By successfully promoting internal stability and progress, he re-established Austria on the world stage, was instrumental in settling the Southern Tirol issue with Italy, helped to set up the European Free Trade Association and proposed a type of Marshall Plan for the Third World.

We set off for Vienna by train, a long journey made more memorable by a prolonged stop in Cologne at night and the misfortune of being directed to a wrong connecting train and having to reach Vienna through the Russian sector.

Arriving in Cologne in the middle of the night was quite eerie. The main railway station is situated below the famous Dome and there was as yet no roof over the platforms. It was a moonlit night and we could clearly see the monumental church building standing erect and apparently undamaged in the midst of total destruction. It was a stark reminder of the calamity Germany had brought upon herself.

I have already commented on the illogicality of calling the most famous Vienna sausage a 'Frankfurter'. The Germans know better and call it 'Wienerli'. Anyhow, when we crossed the border into Austria and stopped in Salzburg station, my first thought was a pair of my favourite Frankfurters on a cardboard tray with lots of mild mustard and a crusty roll, as sold from mobile buffets at railway stations. Sure enough, I was able to purchase this icon of Austrian fast food cuisine by lowering the compartment window, but only to be disappointed by flavour and texture. So many years had passed – had my voracious, youthful appetite deceived me or was I eating post-war 'Ersatz' sausages? After this first experience, they never tasted as good as I had remembered as a child.

From Salzburg the train continued to the nearby railway junction of Hof, where we were due to take a connection to Vienna via Linz, thus entering the capital from the West through the American sector. Unfortunately, two connecting trains were waiting and in the confusion caused by crowds and language problems, we were directed to the wrong train. It was destined for Klagenfurt in the southern province of Carinthia, which meant that we had to take another train from there to take us to Vienna, entering the town through the Russian sector. No problem with a British passport you may say, but it was rather like going through 'Checkpoint Charlie' as set up by the East German communist government in Berlin. Officious, nit-picking and often menacing Russian officers would hold up trains for hours in the blind exercise of their powers. We were relatively lucky to be on our way again after two hours of questioning and searching.

We arrived in Vienna's southern terminal station just six hours later than planned. We had phoned from Klagenfurt and my uncle was there to meet us. I was soon re-united with my aunt and my girl cousin. Gerda was now an attractive 20-year-old whom I had last seen in the Austrian countryside thirteen years earlier. Her mother had lost neither her good looks nor the high-spirited characteristics which carried her and her daughter safely through the Nazi era.

Vienna suffered considerable damage, especially near the end of the war when the Russians fought their way into the city. The State Opera House was a sorry mess of crumbling stone, but this icon of Viennese culture would soon be lovingly rebuilt, long before thousands of homeless citizens could be re-housed.

We stayed with my aunt and uncle for about ten days. Theirs was a typical apartment from pre-WWI, with a long, wide corridor, huge rooms, a bath that was obviously an add-on, and a separate toilet with a lavatory pan that allowed the user to inspect its contents before pulling the chain. I already hated these now obsolescent lavatories when living in the Mariannengasse. They were made worse by the awful paper one had to use.

Our time in Vienna was filled with visits to old landmarks such as the Kahlenberg in the Vienna Woods with its panoramic restaurant. There, when growing impatient after a long wait, we were told by our waiter, *"Alles mit der Ruhe, wir wollen Mensch bleiben,"* which could be translated as "Relax, we want to stay human." Later, after we had ordered some roast beef, he came back with the message, *"Mein Herr, das Fleisch ist noch nicht gut abgelegt",* "Sir, the meat has not been hung enough." After this exchange, I knew that I was well and truly in the Vienna I had known – albeit one that was still in the grip of austerity.

There was one typical example of the Viennese sense of humour. The day after the Russians unveiled a memorial near the city centre featuring a larger-than-life soldier, a watch appeared on the statue's wrist and a fountain pen was stuck on the tunic pocket! After capturing the town, Russian soldiers had gone on the rampage for three days. They took every watch and pen they could lay their hands on, whilst on a general looting and raping spree!

We visited the elegant Hotel de France on the Ringstrasse and were treated to a substantial complimentary Sunday brunch, plus an invitation to their out-of-town hotel, the Panhans. This, then famous hotel was situated on the Semmering, a mountain resort south of Vienna and still a popular destination during the hot summers of the Danube basin. Both hotels were again in the hands of their pre-war owners who were distant relatives of my grandparents – hence the generous hospitality.

Vienna is a seductive town and post-war conditions could not diminish its strong appeal. The outward charm of its inhabitants, its treasures and traditions, the music, the surrounding villages where

'Heuriger', the new wine, is served in a most sociable atmosphere to the strains of *'Schrammelmusik'* and, above all, the untranslatable *'Gemütlichkeit'* – that feeling of comfort and conviviality that seems always to prevail.

But a visit to my uncle's lawyer broke the spell. I was made to feel deeply ashamed of indulging in unfettered enjoyment since coming to Vienna. Now I was to be confronted by official declarations of the deaths of mother, grandmother and great-grandmother, and by the prospect of an inheritance emerging from the slaughter of Hitler's genocide against the Jews.

After I had signed the necessary Powers of Attorney and various other documents, I was told that I was now entitled to an advance on the eventual sale of the private mansion at Mariannengasse 3. I did not question the mechanism that produced this welcome payment – perhaps it came from a government hardship fund? Instead, I decided there and then that I would sell my share of the leather button business to my junior partner on terms he could afford, and join Viki in London for good.

It seems appropriate at this point to end the biographical part of 'My Mother was Viennese', because what followed in the subsequent sixty years is a relatively uneventful story of a young man embarking on a fresh career path with enough success to ensure a comfortable retirement. It is also the not uncommon story of a sometimes bumpy, childless marriage that nevertheless lasted 58 years – 62 years in all of togetherness, from first acquaintance at the Carl Bryant School of Dancing in Surbiton, Surrey, to a sad farewell at the Barlavington Nursing Home near Petworth in West Sussex.

As a naturalized British citizen since 1947, I have always taken pride in being British. Sometimes, I am saddened by what is happening in 'my' country, because I want it to be always the best in the world. I have a deep feeling of gratitude and have spent the last few years giving back what I can to a country that has given me safety, freedom and the opportunity to succeed in life.

Käthe Caliò, the friend in Italy who sheltered my mother when she fled from Vienna, and who was the first in January 1946 to tell me of her fate, continued to write to me until 1967, the year she died. Her letters, which are largely reproduced in Part IV, are full of remorse for not doing more to protect my mother from arrest and deportation. They also give an insight into the misery of her own life during those post-war years. Käthe is one of the subjects of Professor Crosina's research into the fate of the Jews in Northern Italy, and I have included some of the material in Part III, The Testimony.

Before World War I. The Austro-Hungarian Empire in 1914.

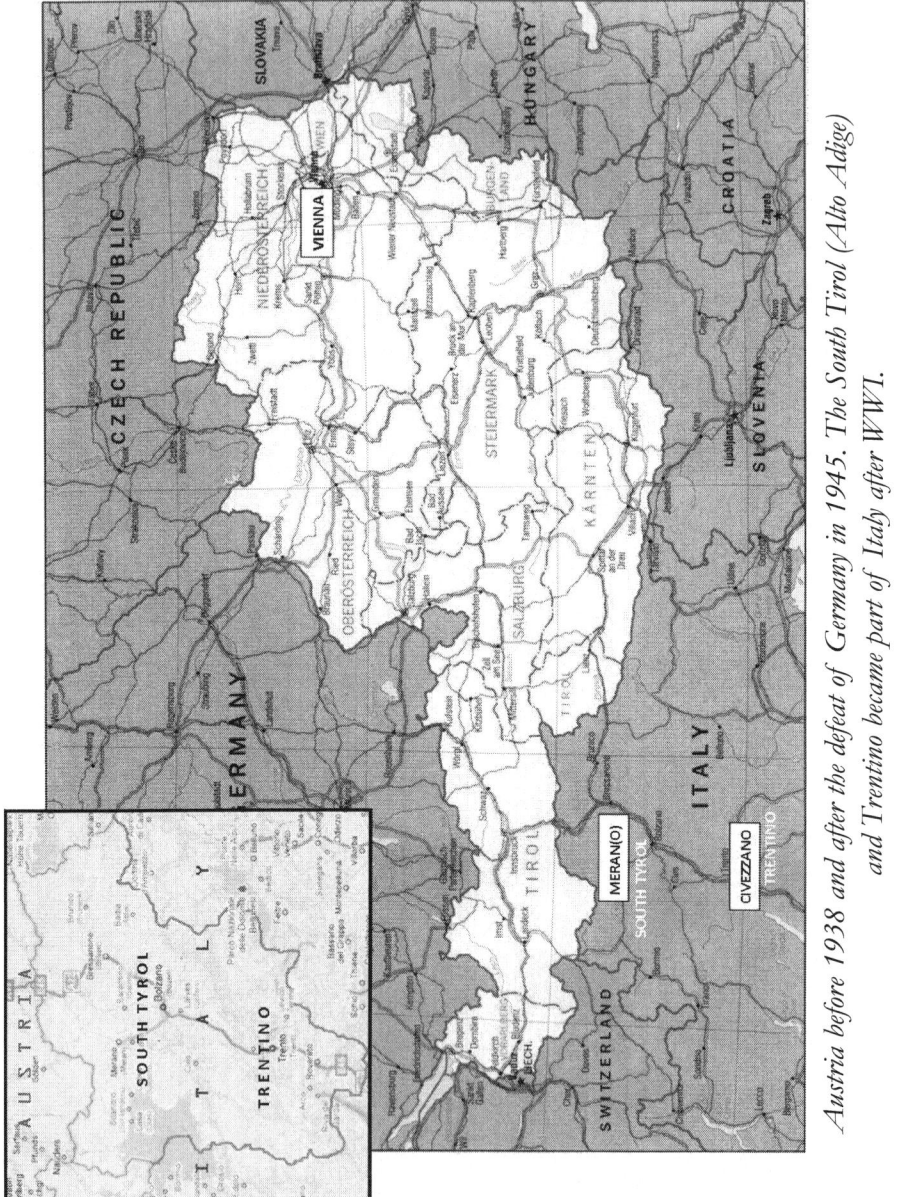

Austria before 1938 and after the defeat of Germany in 1945. The South Tirol (Alto Adige) and Trentino became part of Italy after WWI.

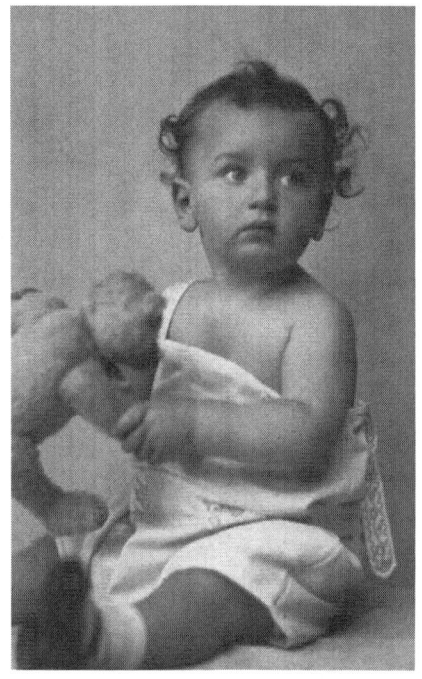

Mummy's darling at one-year-old

First love in Paris? 1929

With my great-grandmother in our garden, 1928

With Mother, 1932

In Meran, 1930

With Mother in Meran, 1930/31

With Mother in Paris, 1929

My Father, 1920

My German passport issued in Vienna on 19th September 1938. Three days later I arrived at Croydon airport after a seven-hour flight. The Frankfurt Border Control stamp meant freedom. No 'J' appeared in the passport.

St Marylebone Grammar School Brass Band in Redruth, Cornwall, 1941. Who bangs the big drum?

With Viki in 1945

With Käthe Caliò and her daughter Tea in 1953

Tea Caliò cuts the cake with her bridegroom Rocco in 1967

Professor Maria Luisa Crosina with Signor Vielmetti, who translated from Italian into German for me.

The Memorial lit for Holocaust Day 2011. Representatives of many local authorities light candles and the Arco Councillor for Culture lays a fresh stone each year as a signal of perpetual rememberance.

PART II – A MOTHER'S DIARY

Introduction

May I leave Peter's notebook with you for the time being? I can't take it with me. Perhaps you will read a few lines occasionally and when it's over, will ask you for it. Please don't be angry.

With this note, hurriedly written in pencil on a scrap of paper, my mother sent her diary of my early childhood years to the conductor Willem van Hoogstraaten, prior to fleeing Vienna and eventually seeking refuge high up on a mountain in the Italian province of Alto Adige, with Käthe, her good friend from student days.

In a letter to me dated 31st October 1949, which I have included, van Hoogstraaten tells how it got into his possession and gives some indication of his relationship with my mother. Nevertheless, that relationship and the ending of her note remain an enigma. Why should he be angry, be upset?

I finally received the diary in June 1950 whilst I was living and working in South Wales.

I have not made style or idiom my priorities in the English version. Instead, I have tried to convey the meaning of what my mother said, as faithfully as possible. Observing a child aged from three to twelve inevitably includes a few virtually untranslatable entries such as mispronunciations and malapropos, which I did not attempt to translate. As the diary progresses, the entries get less frequent whilst, at the same time, my mother's comments increasingly illuminate our relationship, the good and not so good in my character and her attitude towards me and to life in general.

82 years have passed since my mother began writing the diary. It is my most prized possession. It tells me so much about the mother I left and lost before I could really get to know her – her humanity, decency, compassion and her remarkable insight into human nature and the mind of a child.

Above all, the pages of the diary are imbued with a mother's deep love for her son.

Translation of Letter from Willem Van Hoogstraaten

Hotel Ketterer
Stuttgart
31.10.49

Dear Peter, an old friend of your dear mother is writing these lines. Käthe C. gave me your address.

Many years ago your mother gave me a diary; she wrote it in the very first years of your youth. It contains mainly thoughts about you and your sayings as a small child. She asked me to guard this book. I managed to save it, even though our apartment was plundered in 1945. It is now in Tutzing in Upper Bavaria and I can only retrieve it personally. I do want to send it to you but fear it <u>could</u> get lost. Also, I am not sure if I have your correct address. You and I, dear Peter, met briefly at Elmau, and I believe, also in Munich.

I knew your mother when she was 17-18. We wrote occasionally to each other over many years. I do not have these letters any more, as I am in the habit of tearing up everything personal. I must have been 33-36 years-old that time at Castle Elmau. I can still see Eva clearly in front of me today and hear the voice with its Viennese intonation. At that time she read a lot of Dostoyevsky and talked about him with great admiration. Every conversation with her went straight into profound depths. She had such a clear understanding, such an uncanny grasp of what was essential. Rarely have I got to know so dear, so wonderful a human being.

Half my life now lies inbetween. I cannot give you any details, but I can say one thing, that it was always a joy for me to speak to her and to hear from her by letter.

How may things be with you, Peter? If you prefer to write in English, that's fine with me. I spent 18 years in America.

Shall I try to send you the folder when I am in Tutzig over Christmas? Or shall I send it to Käthe?

It would be nice to have a letter from you.

I am the conductor here of the *Stuttgarter Philharmoniker*.

I hope you have a fulfilled life and that you are well.

With my sincerest wishes, your old friend, Willem van Hoogstraaten.

A Mother's Diary

Peter

Vienna 31st August 1928

3 Years and 2 months old.

Peter has returned from a summer holiday and has been given malted milk to drink. He does not want it, but I insist. "How was it?" "I have to think about that" – long pause – "now I know how milk with malt tastes in Vienna, it was q-u-i-t-e good."

"To-morrow I will be very good; to-morrow all naughtiness has already run away."

"Please be so good and give me a lot of bread and butter."

He is being washed and suddenly laughs. "What is it?" "I am laughing about something else. I like the trees in the Rathauspark" (Town Hall Park).

In the tram Peter studies an old lady who has nodded off. Suddenly, in a loud voice: "I'll sleep as well now." And in a shop he shouts and laughs: "I know Millstadt!"

1st September 1928

Peter ties a string around his middle, "Now I have a stomach armband."

"I need a hammer, I am a judge."

"Will you finish this drink?" "I hope so."

"Come, mama, I want to tidy up your toys."

He puts on a white rowing shirt: "Right, now I am a Mr Bath Attendant, but the one who gets the money."

"Will you be good now?" "Yes, the naughtiness gets into a car and drives away."

"Stop this flattery, from whom did you learn it?" "From the newspaper seller."

In front of a hospital, "What is this? – I think it's a spinach" (Spital/Hospital – Spinach/Spinat).

4th September

How awful the metropolis is for children! What noises, what a plethora of differing impressions! Peter now walks nervously through the streets, pulling and pulling. Let's hurry on, and he is often afraid that cars will mount the pavement. Then he makes fun of himself to overcome his fears. Today, when a large lorry came thundering along, he said, "I'm happy when a car comes and makes so much noise."

He was in ecstasy today at the Strudelhof Steps, the frog at the fountain and the divided staircase, and he called out, "I want to see everything, everything I don't know already!"

And then there are the many beggars and cripples in the town. Should a mere child have to walk past all this misery with indifference and how is it to comprehend that we return to the comfort of our homes without helping? Each time we pass a beggar, Peter says, "Why don't you give him something?"

"Opapa is the friend of Omama, isn't he?" (Granddad and Granny).

6th September

"Mama, did you buy me?" "No, you were a present."

"I am already big, so should I say to you 'Küss die Hand, gnädige Frau' (I kiss your hand, gracious lady) or 'Grüss Gott, Eva Flatter.'"

7th September

A tram is close behind us. Peter keeps getting up and shouting, "Look, mama, he will run into us."

A salesman speaks to Peter in a department store: "Are you a girl?" "No, but I would like to be a girl." "Why is that?" "Well, why always a boy?" Then he says to the salesman, "Have you time? Come, we will get into an airship and travel far away."

Due to a little accident, his trousers are wet. "Well," he says, "that can happen to children."

Suddenly he starts to berate his elephant, "You must do it, what did I tell you only the day before yesterday?"

"Mama, give me a Pleblauer (Preblauer Mineral Water), when I was small I always said Ple-blau-er."

"And what do you say now?" "Pleblauer!"

8th September

"Papa, why are you a painter?"

"When I'm grown up, I will go to the lavatory too. I will tell my children: 'I'll be back soon, I am going to the loo'."

"Are your eyes blue too?" "Who told you, your eyes are blue?" "The flowers." "How do the flowers speak?" "Like a wolf."

At the table: "Just a moment, I'm thinking about something." "You can do that later in bed." "What, the same as now?" "Alright, what was it?" "Whether the flowers are still beautiful?"

"I would like to be grown up, then one doesn't have to eat any more. But you, mama, must still be with me when I grow up."

11th September

Peter is pulling faces in front of a mirror. Suddenly, he calls, "Come here, I will show you a face you don't know. Look (he puts on a very friendly face), you see when one pulls a face like this, one can only say nice things," and then he addresses me, full of benevolence, with a few sentences.

Peter will always have to be kept in check to calm his listlessness. He has great difficulty controlling his dark moods.

18th September

I reprimand him. "What punishment do you deserve?" "An English one."

"Look, something has bitten me. Perhaps it is a mosquito that has come by train from Millstadt."

Speaking to himself, he says, "Peter, leave that, leave it, leave it!" Then he turns to me: "You know I always obey."

"Mama, it's so-o-o nice in your bed. I am always 'bedding' that you let me join you."

Peter is dancing. "What are you doing?" "A little French and a little English."

He comes into a shop and says, "There is a very nice shop next door."

19th September

Peter doesn't stop talking during afternoon tea. Suddenly, he says, "Why do you let me talk so much during tea?"

"I once saw a child that was <u>very</u> good."

"What do you think you are doing running to another floor alone?" "I thought: who lives here?"

He remembers hurting his little cousin on Sunday and announces it thus: "It's not true at all; I did not hurt Bobby on Sunday at all."

There is some soot in the milk. "That's nothing, is it; somebody put it in to make it taste better, didn't they?"

As we pass a dairy, he says with disgust, "It is unbelievable; some people drink their milk in the street."

He says to a dummy, "You are making an intolerable noise."

"Papa will be coming home." "Is it Sunday today, is the studio locked up?"

"I'm dirty here, wipe it off, wipe the whole person off, the body and everything that belongs with it!"

"You must not tread on the carpet." "It's new isn't it and freshly painted?"

The electrician has arrived to repair a socket. Peter closes the door, having fled into another room. "I don't want to see what coat he is wearing."

8th October

"The lamp has got a new umbrella."

"The string won't come down, Jesus Christ!"

"When I hear the church bells, I ask myself, 'What on earth is ringing'?"

Crossing the road, I say to him, "Quickly, we don't want to get run over." Peter: "We still want to live."

21st November

Peter is sitting on his chamber pot for serious business. "Look," he says afterwards in earnest contemplation, "how nice, I have done something really practical today."

Peter: "Look, my child, it's not so simple."

He hit me in the face today, but showed such heartfelt regret that I was quite amazed: "Look, I so-o-o wish I had not done it," and he sobs and cries; for the first time not out of fear of punishment, but out of pain for having hurt me. "When will it be alright again?" and there was no end to the affection he showed me.

4th December

"May I run the water?" "No, you were naughty and you can only do that as a reward." "I would rather that it is a punishment which has to be observed."

14th December

"That's mine." "How do you know that?" "Because I have good eyes."

Peter is playing conductor: "Where are you going?" "To war."

"Something really horrible!" He can't get enough of stories which entertain by instilling fear.

Whilst shopping, I am given a lot of small change. "Did you buy money?"

25th December

He praises a toy he has received for Christmas: "You see, this one is something quite delightful."

He calls the Christmas Stollen a Wiener Schnitzel and in the night, after an exiting evening, he calls out in his sleep, "Look mami!"

He does something silly and wants me to do it as well. When I fail, he commands, "Then go back to school and learn it!"

He plays at being a schoolboy and has returned from the school. "What did you learn?" "To empty chamber pots!"

I wanted to awaken in him a sense of the joy of giving and allowed him, with the help of Frau Marie, to make little gifts for everyone. They were all placed in a large box and he was jubilant when I brought it into the Christmas room and he could hand a present to each of us.

He gets mixed up between the familiar 'Du' and the more formal 'Sie'. He does seem more stupid now than he was and can't even count any more. But I'm quite happy about that. Let him absorb what he needs organically. It's no use cramming knowledge into children. Real understanding must be preceded by need.

1st January 1929

He says, "You know, being ever-so-careful is something really dreadful."

I'm already in my overcoat and want to go out with him. When I urge him to get ready, he says in a comforting voice, "Don't worry; it will only take another two to three hours."

Peter wants to know where one was before appearing on earth and where one gets to when no longer on it. Also what does "to have died" mean and how long will he remain on earth.

Yesterday he was suddenly delighted that I sit on my "popo" (bottom).

He is now very fearful, asks in the evening when I will be lying in my bed next to his and whether I will be staying the whole night. During the night he wakes with a start and asks anxiously, "Mama, is it morning soon?"

Otto has now been away for five weeks. During the day, Peter doesn't notice his absence, but when we return for a walk in the evening and pass through the anteroom, he says, "There's no overcoat." When dreaded night descends, he wants his loved ones around him. He too feels we need protection and asks, "Why is he leaving us alone?"

You may well ask why, my dear child!

4th January

He often hears about putting on weight and slimming, and says, "I am ill, I have been slimmed."

"Does the cow lay milk?" "No, it is milked." "Does that hurt her?"

He shows great interest in unfortunates of every kind, beggars, invalids, cripples. He wants to know about the nature of their suffering and cannot be diverted from his questioning, given that he sees so much misery on the streets.

8th January

We enter a shop. The salesman is bent over and writing, all we see is a shiny bald head. Peter calls out aloud, "Look mama, the man has nothing on his head, not even <u>one</u> hair, at least Opapa has a few." Service was not of the best.

"You know, I can already read." "Where did you learn it?" "I conjured it into my head."

Peter talks to the elderly caretaker: "When one gets as old as this, one no longer understands everything."

I meet him in the street; it is very cold and he needs his nose wiped frequently. "Mama," he shouts across the road, "I have water in the nose today!"

He assures me, "Really, you can believe me."

He invents a thousand stories and muddles reality and fantasy. If he is denied something because he has misbehaved, he straight away tells of a child which was also naughty, but still got everything it wanted.

He is beginning to sing, draw and wants to know about cause and effect.

For some time now he has been occupied with all kinds of variations of the saying, "When one has something, one does not have it after all." Today I told him, "If you have an apple, you can eat it and it is then in your stomach." But he stayed with, "I have it and I don't have it," and he explained his thesis thus: "I can't eat the whole apple, I would not be able to digest it all – so I don't have it."

26th January

Peter plans to go to a ball with Frau Marie when he grows up, but she tells him that she would be an old hag by then. That interests Peter enormously: "How will you look, how tall will you be and what can one give you for it?"

His Aunt Lisle laughs a lot. Peter says, "She likes to live."

The snowy weather is wild and fun. Peter was out with his toboggan and was really enjoying himself. He laid back and cried, "I am so happy, I am so happy!" Slowly he is also taking pleasure in making things; he perseveres to the end and is proud and delighted when he can show the result. But the "I can't" has to be overcome first.

I am now much calmer and more even-tempered with him and try to help him get over his moods and ill humour by making fun and keeping him occupied, instead of reacting with irritability as I used to.

He says to himself, "It's really dreadful, the way I behave sometimes."

May 1929

"When I go for a walk," says Peter "the Dear Lord always sends me a rattle. But today I was good, today he needed it himself."

I bought a small bird. It was grey, had a red beak and came in a small wooden cage which was easy to handle. I wanted to give Peter something to look after, something to worry about. However, it died after a week and I only found out afterwards that this species only thrives as a pair. The bird was called 'Little' and it was so sad when it no longer hopped around, stopped eating, tucked its little head into its feathers, quivered and passed away. Peter did not understand, he laughed and looked forward to cleaning the cage.

He takes great interest in the body's natural functions: "Look, I have eaten a banana and now it is in my (chamber) pot." And on another occasion: "Making ca-ca happens to be my purpose in life."

On the 2nd May the Zeppelin (airship) flew over Vienna. Like everyone else, Peter was at the window, but was scared and greatly relieved that it was only visible from a distance.

(Since then, the Zeppelin had to abort a flight to America and had to land on the French coast with faulty engines and a Mistral wind threatening to break it up).

Peter is frightened by all sorts of things. Suddenly he has a horror of flies. Before going to sleep he torments me with hundreds of reasons for bringing me back into the bedroom. Sometimes he hallucinates slightly and wants to say "good night" countless times. I try not to get angry on these occasions, but I will on no account encourage these obsessive ideas.

The mouthwash is too strong. Peter says, "It blinds me."

Aunt Lisle attends an evening course in law. Peter wants an explanation, then interrupts me: "Well, they all sit together and the teacher says to one of them, 'Do you want to learn with me?'"

"Is the popo (bottom) cut with a knife?"

I want to give Peter cheese for supper, but he wants milk as well and says very seriously as justification, "I have two hungers."

Yesterday he was conscious for the first time of having had a dream and was able to describe it. He rubbed his eyes, stretched and said, "Mama, I had a dream. The Dear Lord descended from heaven on a ladder, came to the Mariannengasse and rang the bell. Then he came in and tied a small balloon to my bed, it was so small like a baby. And now I have woken up and can see it was only a dream."

I noticed from his account that he dealt with the Dear Lord – with whom he feels mighty uneasy because "He sees everything" – in a natural way. I was pleased that he had Him ringing the doorbell and not flying in through the window.

His grandmother often reads him stories, but I have now asked her to stop because they leave him full of anxieties. She is concerned about his education, but I am not at all anxious as to whether he can tell the time or knows a thousand things.

This year Peter associates staying in the countryside with something pleasurable and is looking forward to enjoying the freedom of the woods and meadows. If he stays fit, I expect it will have a calming influence on his poor city nerves and prove an enlivening experience for him.

6th June

Peter asks how children suddenly appear. When one refers him to the Dear Lord who sends them to two people who love each other he has, as expected, a thousand questions. How is it the Dear Lord has enough bones and how does he throw the children to earth, etc.?

Then he asks what the two "skin buttons" (nipples) are for. In fact, he asks continuously and the way he dispatches the questions is ugly. Constantly answering does not make sense either. If possible, he should find out that his own observations and strange experiences should alternate.

Nowadays he often gives things a name and treats the words and expression with loving care. When he is full of life, the ordinary term will not do, and he embellishes it with all kinds of diminutives and endearments. The feared fly is a "Surli" etc.

When he is in this state, everything is dear to his heart and he cries over every piece of paper snatched from his tender care. On one of these occasions he proposed taking the house into the country by first dismantling and then assembling it there, so that it would not be left on its own.

21st August

Peter is too much amongst grown-ups and has got into the habit of making conversation. But it is my wish that he should develop organically, that his knowledge increases slowly through questions he really needs to ask. Education should not be through a plethora of data, it should be a personal development from inside. Almost everyone handles children like dolls – it is particularly noticeable during the summer holidays. In the same way as people do not spare woods and meadows, leaving them defiled, so they insist on inhibiting the lives of their children, to civilize them as much as possible. But it is culture that matters, not civilization.

Peter calls, "Quickly, mama, see what's going on; there are so many people standing around, that must be a celebration or an accident."

He calls a dense forest a "Spike forest."

There are many Polish Jews here in Gräfenberg. I notice that Peter gesticulates with his hands when he talks. When I object, he says: "I am a pupil, so I'm allowed to speak with my hands."

The cook in our pension complains that the owner is very unpleasant and never takes a step out of the kitchen. When Peter met the lady in the corridor and she greeted him, he became quite exited and shouted: "Look, she has stepped out."

There was a heavy thunderstorm and the lights went out whilst Peter was having his supper. He was very upset and now wants to go to bed without his supper, so that his eyes "will be closed before it gets dark again."

He is receiving a short course of treatment in the sanatorium here, consisting of a hip bath every second day. On sunny days I send him to a spring in the woods, where he can first play naked and then splash around in it to his heart's content. He is often extremely wild and unmanageable and needs real work to absorb his energy. I want to encourage him to listen, to look at the trees, the flowers, the animals in the forest. I bought him a standard Fuchsia hoping that he will care for it himself – this is more important than learning poems by heart. Observing things may lead him away from self-centeredness, something that affects every single child.

I do not want to choose his company for him any more than I will be persuaded as to whom I should associate with. A child from the 'best home', constantly supervised and over-civilized, is much less to my liking than a simple child of simple, kind-hearted parents.

22nd November

Peter is beginning to show an interest in the clock, he asks the time frequently and how long it will be before it is such and such. However, five minutes and three hours are often all the same to him.

In the morning he often wakes very early, when I am still far from awake. So I thought of a way of keeping him quiet: I appoint him as 'sleep-commandant', which makes him very proud. Then when he becomes restless again, I demote him, because 'he is not worthy'. This makes him cry and shout, "re-appoint me, re-appoint me!"

He now goes to a gym and has been there twice. The need to fit in will be good for him and a preparation for school. At the moment he talks constantly and disturbs the other children. He came back from his first hour there very proudly and reported, "The teacher said 'You are praised, you are praised and you are praised'" – in short, he was among them.

14th March 1930

This year Peter was dressed as a *Krampus* devil. It made him very happy when one was oh-so scared of him. Actually, we had no choice because he first went up to each of us with the urgent request to "be really frightened!"

He wants to dance. Frau Marie suggests he should take her to a ball. Peter says, "You know, the ball can't be quite round, otherwise people couldn't dance."

He sees a veiled lady and is appalled at her "grille" and that if she sneezes, everything "is dirty."

Much of what Peter thinks and asks has to do with truth and death. Very often he says "it's not true" and it pleases him to cheat so that he can say afterwards that it wasn't the truth at all.

He wants to know how long one is here and what happens when one isn't here any more, whether one still digests etc., and he uses the word death very often.

I see it more and more clearly: Peter needs an organized, cheerful environment, as much objectivity as possible must surround him – order, activity and positive individuals.

He was in the exhibition pavilion with his grandmother. There he met a robot who spoke to him. That really occupied his mind and the following morning he awoke with the words:, "I have a lot to tell you, mama."

15th March

In the mornings Peter always pays me a short visit in my bed. Sometimes he conjures something away or he pretends to have done something forbidden so that he can tell me later that it wasn't true. To day we talked about a future occupation. He declared that he would only learn what he wanted, such as musician or chauffeur and he let me list various professions before commenting: "You know, it is the Dear God who forces one to become what one wants to become."

Peter tells me with sparkling eyes that he will become a soldier, so he can always jump to "attention."

Often he tells me what he will do when he is grown-up and how it will all be. And being grown-up is often connected to food, for instance: "I will order a tea and will have whatever I want with it, perhaps lemon."

Sometimes he can be very affectionate and then again all closeness can be repulsive to him. When he hops into bed with me in the morning and has slept well, he loves to caress me. "That's my little head, it belongs to me," and he embraces my neck and sings the words to me.

The other morning we were out walking. Peter played with a little boy. When I called him to go home, he did not want to leave the little one because he was alone in the park. He showed himself to be very concerned and especially caring. "If your father doesn't come," Peter said to him "and you have to go home on your own, you must always wait until everybody crosses the road and then you can go too." Later he asked if he could go back to have a look and accompany the boy if no-one had fetched him.

I wondered how my little counsellor would have behaved if <u>he</u> had been left alone in the park, but I was pleased that he showed such concern.

11th April

Peter wants to buy a lottery ticket and ask if he can buy one in the chemist's shop.

He sees and hears a lot of advertising and asks, often in the case of deathly earnest matters, whether it is publicity.

Peter wants to go to a coffee house. When he wants something, he doesn't hesitate to find ways and means to achieve it. It starts to drizzle, straightaway he comes with the threat that there will probably soon be a rainstorm – something that sounded very amusing coming from him.

The actor Emil Jannings was in Vienna and was given an over-enthusiastic reception. He even suffered injuries. Peter is often out and about and actually witnessed this storm of adulation. Today, he asked whether Hoch-Jannings would come again, believing that was his name <u>(Hoch</u> – a toast).

Peter says with emphasis and comic indignation, "What shall I do then, shall I laze about?"

He says: "Please save this for me, otherwise the Dear Lord will be angry."

"You do everything wrong, you are a bad joke."

"Shall we play salesman?"

He is now quite *au fait* with the clock and consequently asks again and again what time it is. Sometimes he wakes in the night: "Mama, what time is it?"

He has a cold and I try to explain to him that it is necessary to get rid of the phlegm. "If I'm allowed to spit, I would rather do it in the street."

He was physically quite aggressive and I suggest that he apologizes. "I won't do it, I'm ashamed."

He often expresses the wish to go into a church. I took him on two occasions; the first visit was quite short and he did not sense the mystery. The second time, he asked to stay for longer. I had said no to whether one <u>had</u> to pray. We sat down on two chairs; Peter was very quiet, "You know," he said suddenly "I am not doing what one does when praying." This was followed by a faltering pause with which he seemed to indicate that something of the sort did stir within him. He was very still and solemn, not wild and unruly as is usual when he is exhorted to be quiet. It was very pleasant.

14th April

Exceptionally, Peter is having breakfast with his grandmother and drinks his milk like a good boy. She tells him she will tell Frau Marie that he is the best-behaved boy in Vienna. Peter is greatly touched by this. With tears in his eyes and stretching every word, he stammers: "But-she-will-not-believe-you."

He says, "A person looks like their name." He probably thinks that, because the name reminds him of the person.

Travelling with him by tram or worse, by metro, is quite an experience. While waiting for the train, Peter keeps a wary eye on my hands; woe betide me if, at the terrifying moment of boarding, I should take a handkerchief out of my bag or do something equally dangerous which could imperil getting on safely. We have to stand exactly on the spot where the train will arrive and are not even allowed to shift from one foot to the other, anything else brings tears to his eyes and his voice and hands tremble.

When at last the train arrives, we have to board with lightening speed and must remember to stand ready by the exit no less than a quarter of an hour before we need to get off.

These are the anxieties that beset Peter. There is no sense in talking about it to him; when he discovers the ease with which such tasks can be accomplished and has to face the difficulties of so many other things in life, these little gremlins will disappear.

Peter often promises to marry Frau Marie. But when he misbehaves and she rebukes him, he becomes very quiet and says ponderously, "I will have to consider carefully whether I want you as my wife."

Peter wants some Easter cake. I ask him when he would like to eat it. "As a starter, after the meal."

The tracks of the trams are being repaired and there are notices to that effect. Peter draws my attention to the 'recipe'. A theatre programme is also a 'recipe'.

12th May

Yesterday was Mother's Day. Peter worked on a picture for me. He cut out flowers which Frau Marie glued on and the picture now hangs in its frame from the lamp over my bed. He outdid himself in praising it: how beautiful, wonderful, lovely. He has a savings bank which he opened and felt obliged to sacrifice a shilling for Mother's Day and to buy some tulips with it. These too were beautiful, wonderful and lovely.

For him, it was a big day yesterday, not because it belonged to his mother, but because it was his first visit to a theatre. I took him and his grandmother to a children's revue, organized by a children's group. The progamme was fun and really devised for a young audience. Through a series of scenes, it presented a day at the holiday camp. Peter was much taken with it, applauded and did not get over-excited, which I feared would have been the case at a real theatre performance. The experience has created a bridge to movement, colour, language and music.

13th May

Today we went to a swimming bath for the first time. The establishment bears the name of the goddess Diana, the *Dianabad*. Peter, not knowing the goddess, calls it *Indianerbad*. Needless to say, he had never seen so many naked and half-naked bodies; in Millstadt he was still too young to have noticed. He was so distracted by the nudity that he could not dress himself and it was a miracle that he managed to do it in the end without once looking.

The water was not new to him. The lower diving board was simply the diving board, but the higher one was a "somersault board." On the way home we played "swimming instructor."

After the bath, I bought him some quality cakes, which he found "so good as to be crazy about."

17th May

Peter was at the circus. I was not with him. Apparently he was not nervous and enjoyed everything hugely. In the evening he cried out in his sleep and reports in the morning that he is always dreaming about the lady whose neck got longer and longer. He is a realist and always wants to know how it is done, but without loosing his enthusiasm.

He says, "You can come too, you are ticketed."

Sometimes he says to me: "I love my mama" – and at that moment, he believes it. But the next morning he assures Frau Marie with great sincerity that "today I love you more than ever before," and that this "will last until I die."

Then he announces his intention to live for very long and to master many occupations such as musician, policeman, builder and so on.

Peter is still not really familiar with clocks, but always wants to know what time it is and how long before he can get up, etc. A half hour is too long for him, two quarter hours are more acceptable, and he laughs with pleasure when something is only going to take three or ten minutes.

He was very amused yesterday when with a hot sun in the sky, he called out, "Now all the icemen have gone," and I replied they are now "hotmen."

It is also very nice today and Peter went out into the sun highly elated. When Frau Marie came he thanked her quite in earnest for the good weather, to which she said she was not St Peter. Whereupon he wanted to play St Peter and Frau Marie had to be Dear God and thank him for the good weather.

24th May

He was at a funeral with my mother. Such an event provides him with masses of material for play. He takes a bright red ribbon and says he has a death band and goes looking for a corpse and asks, "Will you be my corpse?" Then he is a gravedigger and buries people. He says he finds it all very amusing.

He no longer wants to eat at the table alone: "I need someone who eats as well."

25th May

Peter likes smelling – his favourite smell is the billiard room. It has a kind of stale, not-lived-in aroma, which he finds delicious. He closes the door behind him and says he must penetrate deeply into the room where he savours the scent alone.

A warm sunny May air is streaming into our room today. Peter says, "It smells hot, it smells of sun."

2nd June

These days I am making frequent excursions with Peter. Today we were in Altenberg on the Danube. He said, "Look, I cannot and cannot believe that we are now so far away, but you know, I can smell it." There is so much to see, to hear and not least, to smell, that all unruliness and sulkiness are exorcised.

30th October

It is now six months since my last entry into Peter's book. There was not enough restful time. We left on 21st June and stayed six weeks in Zoute in Belgium, then six weeks with Dr Müller in Ellmau, one day in Munich, three weeks in Stuttgart, two days in Heidelberg, eight days in Frankfurt/Main and now it is our fifth day in Geneva. I do not want to spend the winter in Vienna, I am looking for modest accommodation and some work, if possible.

Peter has seen and heard a lot. The need now is to organize the winter so that he can experience tranquility, order and homeland. Wherever we might be, he should have the opportunity to digest his impressions and to convert them into a little knowledge, all without being overwhelmed. Somewhere he must feel calm in spite of everything and the only way to contribute to that is through stability, moderation and order.

In Ellmau he found his first friend, a very wild boy to whom he clung more than to other children. His name was Heinz Peters and their parting was, at that moment, quite difficult.

He acquires dialects and odd foreign words very quickly. Languages will come easily to him, but then children always learn faster.

He is continually asking questions. All things technical interest and please him: railway, car, machines – just like all children. He loves to be in the countryside, but always thinks he is not there yet. "Let's go further into the meadow, deeper into the woods," when we are already in the deepest part. He now handles flowers and animals more gently than before; instead, his wild behaviour is directed at me and other people. Actually he does not like to be rough with me; I am straightaway his "Little man" again and he can't stand it when one is angry with him.

We took little Heinz to the Odenwald-School. Peter wanted to stay there.

In Stuttgart we visited the anthropologic open-air school where he chose orange as the colour which indicated his temperament.

Peter also saw a film in Stuttgart called 'Hunting the tiger across India' which he found fascinating. Once again, he was interested mainly in how it was all done – the light, the photography, etc.

In Zoute and in Ellmau he had the company of children. This is important for him, as he must learn to socialize, to fit in, without being weak.

He recently assumed that the "Dear God who sees everything" had closed a trouser button for him, as he could not remember closing it himself. God is often in his thoughts.

Recently, when something had aroused his anger, he advised himself that it would be better if he just felt hurt. (Meaning deep down so that he doesn't notice it at all.)

7th November

For Christmas we want to send home a little parcel of things made entirely from matchboxes.

He presented me with his first drawing today – a vase with flowers.

He wanted desperately to go and feed the swans. There are many wild birds with splendid feathers on the lake here. They often stay for only a few hours. We packed some bread and when I set about feeding them, Peter made a terrible fuss, seeing me already swallowed up.

He is now very pleased when I buy flowers and likes to look after them.

19th November

Peter has now presented me with several pictures, painted or made from cut-outs. He has also drawn the "intestines" of a leaf!

He wants to know the second "catastrophe" of a song and wants to stir the sediment from cocoa. If one involuntarily laughs on such occasions, Peter flies into a rage. Is that the stirrings of ambition? He keeps asking again and again whether something he has made is good, rather good or very good. I always respond to this with praise, but if he were himself convinced, he would proudly stay silent and not press for confirmation.

He is mostly indifferent to kindness or rudeness of people he meets in large numbers in his talkative life. But during the summer he suddenly burst into tears: "None of the children love me, mama."

17th December

Peter overheard me talking about old pictures. That aroused his curiosity and he wants to see "young ones."

He is doing some washing and calls, "I've got it, now I know what a real laundry is like – lots of foam and the water terribly dirty." He does a lot of washing nowadays and aims at imitating a real laundry.

Yesterday, he suddenly said, "Are you mine? My dear, dear little creature. You are so good to me!"

It is now nearly three months since we arrived in Geneva. We are staying in a small hotel and prepare most of our meals on a spirit stove. Peter has settled in and is comfortable here. He has forgotten our various travels, but now has some grasp of geography for which he has undoubtedly some feeling. He speaks of the "farthest land" and of the hot countries which lie on the other side of the earth and he imagines that France, Germany and England are similar. I got a lecture from him explaining how the world came into being, how everything was light and became steadily heavier and that the Dear God was the lightest creature of all.

He would like to have a child and can't understand why he cannot marry one.

A travelling troupe arrived here. They erected a small fairground with many amusements and made a lot of noise. I took Peter there twice. He was very delighted with the carousel, though quite weighed down by the noise, but did not talk about that.

I also took him to see the caravans, the home on wheels of these fairground people, to show him what a hard life they have. Some of them risk their lives every day; there was a demonstration on a motorbike, where a man showed his dangerous skills inside a large metal ball.

We can't visit the swans so often now because it is too cold. Instead, Peter wants to throw them some money so they can buy themselves something.

5th February 1931

We shall be leaving Geneva shortly. My brother has an empty room in Paris and we will stay there. He became father of a baby girl two months ago and Peter looks forward to seeing his little cousin.

It was very quiet and pleasant for him here. A few days ago he caught a fever and had to take to his bed. He is a bit down now and I will make an effort to build him up again.

His reading of printed matter is now quite good and he is busy writing and spelling. He talks about an "R" that can't speak (a mute

R) and asks a lot and gives doctrinaire opinions: "You know, this is so and that is so…" Well, let it be!

"Does the cat lay eggs?" I tell him that she drops a litter, which amazes him and he asks whether it is the same with dogs and other animals, to which he gets a short answer. Then he wants to know how one lays a child or drops or drills it? Or whether one marries one? I would like to tell him that when two people – a man and a woman – love each other, they wish fervently to have a child and because the woman is equipped by nature to raise a child inside her body until it is big enough to survive in the outside world, she does this and gives her husband the child as a present.

And I would not be afraid if more questions arose, because a simple answer about natural things cannot do any harm at any age. But I do not dare to do it yet, because the fact that he no longer believes in Father Christmas has already raised eyebrows.

But not all children are the same. Peter found a Father Christmas that one couldn't see or touch, rather frightening. I also do not want to foist anything about the Christ child on him.

For the time being, I am suppressing my urge to be honest with him and I tell him that one first has to observe and understand the ways of flowers and animals, before one can understand the more complicated human ones. I want to awaken the feeling that the genital organs are a blessing with which he has been entrusted

Yesterday he picked up my diary and found it "nice" that I had saved his pictures in it.

I gave the maid a piece of almond cake yesterday and she explained to him that it is rather rich and that one must not eat too much of it. Peter took the crumb she was still holding, weighed it in his hand and shook his head.

Peter says, "What does fresh air mean? Does God send a different air every few days?"

"It's true isn't it, that mandarins are young oranges?"

27th May

We have now been in Paris for three-and-a-half months. Peter has settled in and has his routine, but it was not easy this time to bring the calm he needs into his life. He is now his blossoming, peaceful self, the way he responds when everything goes smoothly and without excitement.

He says, "o la lá" and parles generally a bit French.

At first, he found the noise deafening, which released all the bad spirits in him and made him very unruly.

There are well-cared-for children of the housekeepers here, with whom he plays frequently. He also has his friends in the various shops we visit and especially in a Russian one, where he is greeted with hallo, lifted up and tossed from one arm to the other.

We will be travelling to Meran in a week's time. He looks forward to the meadows and I to seeing him jumping around on them. There is not much time left before school and this worries me a bit. And yet order is essential for him and, hopefully, he will have more pleasure than stress from the work.

Here, there is now Uncle Benno's baby, which he has to handle gently, something he often finds difficult. Then, there is a cat – Ninette – and in the last few days even a dog. He was a stray, bought cheaply and he was sad and unsociable. He has now been sent into the country.

Peter has affection in him, but has some difficulty expressing and limiting it. It's the same with the cat. He would do everything for it, but he cannot suppress a wild caress and this makes the cat spit at him occasionally. There are also six canaries in the apartment, in which he is not interested because they remain platonically distant – he cannot take them, stroke them or torture with kindness.

The other day, he derived great pleasure from a bunch of lilies of the valley; they brought out the best in him.

Getting him to the table is often difficult. He would sigh, "Mama, I can't stop," and he carries on with whatever he is doing. But this is exactly when I see to it that he does stop. I know that finishing with something is difficult and has to be practiced.

On the 4th of June we travelled to Meran and stayed until the 17th November. Peter spent a lot of time in the open. We returned to Vienna in November and are staying in the parental home.

30.11.1932

Peter has now been going to school for five-and-a-half months. He became ill in Meran with a festering boil and was late starting school, but without missing much, as he was well prepared. Two further illnesses interrupted his schooling (Flu and an ear infection), otherwise he has been stomping to school every morning, his anxieties mingling with curiosity. He leafs through the calendar searching for red days and says he does not 'willingly' go to school. There are duties now, and endless obstacles preventing play.

Large and small print, Latin script, multiplication tables, these are the order – or rather disorder – of the day, as things are still mighty topsy-turvy. The teacher is really quite pleased with his comprehension, but much less so with the lack of order in his work. To produce a page without blots, with reasonably even lettering let alone with even distances between words, makes him suffer torture and is really difficult for him. On top of that, he is very restless. After his illness he had to swallow lots of bromide and at the moment he can't hear properly as the result of the illness. Hopefully this will all soon pass.

He is now getting used to other children and is learning automatically to fit in. His compensation is at home, where he is the centre of attraction and dispenses smiles and displeasure in all directions as he pleases. His cousin, the one-and-a-half-year-old Ditti, does not live here and is not enough of a distraction. He has not yet found any real friends at school, there are some badly neglected children who are aggressive towards him and there are also markedly Jewish children who are very spoilt and have little of benefit to offer him.

He was in the Burgtheater at a play called 'The Dumb Angel' and also in the Raimund- and Volkstheater. The Volkstheater was only a few days ago and the piece was called 'The Easter Hare and the Magic Circle' and it was performed on Easter Sunday. Peter always wants to know how it is all done and whether the people who are beaten up or even die, are as fit as a fiddle afterwards. He comforts me during dramatic scenes, whispering: It's not real, they are only pretending."

I gave him 20 Zehngroschen coins for Easter, which he distributed among the poor. Nowadays one can hardly keep away from beggars, they stand at each street corner offering shoe laces, songs and music – hunger in their eyes, need in their hands – but just on Easter Sunday they all seem to have disappeared . It was quite comical how we went in search of the needy and nearly offered our donation to the wrong people. And when we saw someone suitable in the distance, Peter would run breathlessly across the road towards them, happy to have the opportunity; and if he found him "very poor," he would take two ten Groschen from his purse.

Right now his greatest interest is Christ. We are reading the St Mathew's Passion and when he now discovers that all important public holidays are linked to the person of Christ and that all pictures of saints tell of his work and his death – as gleaned from "our" reading – he is almost filled with pride. If any kind of sugary picture or any equally sanctimonious sculpture can be seen in a shop window, Peter grabs my arm, runs to it and is lost in contemplation: time and time again, it is all about Christ – it seems very strange to him.

Actually, one has to be very careful with him when it comes to miracles and unreal matters, because fear is a ghost with which he has constantly to battle. "Agst" instead of Angst was his first word. I believe he will have enough strength later to combat his weakness, but for the present that firm ground has not been reached – he is swimming in a sea of fear. One example is dreams – he may dream that he has died and is travelling in a hearse. Of late, he has had miserable nights; he cries out and was only comforted when I took him into my bed and watched over him. This has happened quite often, so that he is now afraid to go to sleep.

He has been much weakened by a severe bout of flu and I hope that he will soon, very soon, regain strength. He is starting to read books on his own accord and enjoying them.

He is now so steeped in Christ that he has transformed Radieschen (radishes) into Paradieschen!

A young boy joined us for Easter Monday lunch and stayed the whole afternoon. Then we went to see Buster Keaton in a cinema and Peter was very happy. Yesterday was the last free day, we stayed at home and he and I played a game we called "Entertaining." We decorated the room with paper chains before the "many guests" arrived, Peter at the head carrying a walking stick and hat with which to entertain them. He sat himself down in a large easy chair and read aloud from a book. Then I said goodbye to the guests because Peter had to go to bed, and I asked him to accompany a "Miss Fritzi" home, which he graciously did.

When we are at home in the afternoon, he loves to put on fancy dress. I help him because it gives him innocent pleasure and keeps him busy. His preference is to be a lady and for this he chooses a tight skirt in which he moves with great care taking tiny steps in order not to disturb anything. Normally however, he can hardly keep still for a single moment. Hardly a day passes without some 'disaster'. Yesterday, we had broken plates, a few spilled glasses and a broken clock. He started to swing on the counter-weights and swung so strongly that the clock stopped ticking and the watchmaker had to be called – all that in two minutes!

I help him with his homework and urge him to be tidy, but without fretting about it. What he needs and should absorb, he will grasp slowly from within himself; everything else runs off like water off a waxed surface. The progress I do see: more love for flowers and animals and when there are problems, more will and self-control.

His father collects him every week for a few hours. He has illustrated a book, a bird fable, and has given Peter a copy. Peter proudly shows it to everyone. He is taking a few steps towards becoming a vegetarian, he rejects meat and enjoys oily dishes, salads etc. The doctor says it would be appropriate not to give him meat, which pleased me a great deal and gave me the opportunity to feed him without meat – something that has always been my wish but has met resistance because everyone else in the house eats meat and offers it to him.

During half of our travels he had a vegetarian diet and thrived on it. A lot of vegetables, fruit, cream, light cheese and olive oil. He relished oil with lemon and would dip bread into it. Or a dish we learned in Calabria – bread cooked in oil and garlic. Peter would sleep very well after eating this dish in the evening. Or onions braised in oil, or potatoes with sage. He feels better on a light diet.

When he really wants to please me, he makes the tough decision to discard his feather pillow in favour of a thin horsehair pillow, or he makes do with the mattress and tells me: "I'll sleep without a pillow to-night." He does tend to be very pernickety and has to be kept from too much fussing. For instance, he can't sleep when we are travelling because he doesn't know how he should arrange his bed. He tries desperately, but to no avail! For practice and to harden him for life, he has to make do occasionally without all the cushioning.

I am now going to collect him from school, 11.30 in the morning.

27.11.1935

Peter has so far attended two classes in the elementary school in the Gilgegasse and a third and fourth in the Strassergasse whilst staying at a boarding school in Grinzing.

He is now in the first class of the grammar school in the Glasergasse. He had great difficulty making the transition from the comfortable, peaceful tempo of the elementary school to the more severe and serious environment of the secondary school. Now, after two months, the worst seems to be over. Peter suffers from a mixture of too quick and too slow (the too quick, restless side is in his nerves; the lethargy comes from the body).

When he feels he is under pressure and cannot cope, he responds not with haste in the normal way, no, on the contrary, he resorts to dawdling. It is not something he does intentionally. So far, he has simply not acquired a rapid bodily reaction. I can see from his appearance, lack of appetite and his restless, shallow sleep that he has not yet adapted naturally to the transition.

All of this means that he is constantly stumbling over his own forgetfulness and, as a result, punishment rains down on him. At the very beginning I was asked to see the French teacher who complained bitterly about his behaviour and his forgetfulness. If he does not change, he said, we will not keep him. But I know that the professor (Albrecht) was too gloomy, Peter fits well into any community, he simply had not yet adapted. It is the same with childishness as with haste. Now that he hears from all sides that childishness is no longer acceptable and no longer belongs to the psyche of a secondary school pupil, he is itching and impelled to be childish and is more playful than last year (long may it last!).

Much to my pleasure he is rapidly developing two faculties: keen powers of observation and a three-dimensional concept of shape. He gives his verdict by making comparisons and he compares by observation. If he talks about a machine or the body of an animal or human, I sense that the concept of shape comes naturally to him. Might this gift one day lead to his profession in life or be connected to it in some way? And will it weaken or continue to grow strongly from within?

Ten years of his life have passed. May all that is good accompany him on his way!

His Mother.

Part III – The Testimony

A Tribute

A certificate issued to me on 26th January 1994 by the municipal authorities of the *Commune di Arco* in the Province of Trento, states that my mother was a registered foreigner, resident there from 6.3.1942, "ending on 22.12.1943 because she was arrested by the German authorities."

The information came from the archive of the City of Arco, an ancient town just north of Lake Garda and one of the sources diligently searched by Professor Maria Luisa Crosina for her book *Le Storie Ritrovate* (Rediscovered Histories – Jews in the Province of Trent, 1938-1945). Through her painstaking research Professor Crosina has produced a fully documented testimony of my mother's gruelling final years as a fugitive in Fascist Italy, culminating in her arrest and deportation to Auschwitz.

In her book Professor Crosina also devotes a chapter to my mother's lifelong friend Käthe Caliò (née Perlberg), who sheltered her at a time when it was most needed. Käthe's letters to me after the war revealed much about the mother I never really got to know and of her state of mind during her struggle to survive.

In addition to providing posterity with a record of the fate of Jews resident in the Province of Trent during the Second World War, Professor Crosina initiated a successful campaign to erect a memorial in Arco to the town's three Holocaust victims, of which my mother was one. It was unveiled in December 1993 on the 50th anniversary of the deportations. It consists of a large, rough-hewn piece of Dolomite rock inscribed with the three names and it is set on the edge of a park near the town centre

It was while she was pursuing her research that Professor Crosina discovered my existence by pure chance. A fellow art historian, Dr Dorothea McEwan in London, had published papers about my artist father, J O Flatter, and this led to enquiries about family members of Eva Flatter. From the letters and photographs I was able to provide, and the archive material she had unearthed, Professor Crosina was able to put together the facts and circumstances which make up my mother's chapter in her book. The letters also revealed the role Käthe Caliò played in the story of my mother's flight from Vienna until her tragic end, and this is recorded in another chapter.

Professor Crosina's account inevitably filled me with great sadness and reinforced my feeling of guilt – why did I not do more to save my mother from the terrible suffering she had to endure? But that does not diminish my deep gratitude to her for helping me to follow my mother in spirit during those final years and for producing a permanent record of the evil of Nazi Germany as it reached out into Northern Italy.

'The Testimony' is partly based on Professor Crosina's research and is a record of the final tragic years of my mother's life and the hardship suffered by her closest friend. Two chapters of Professor Crosina's book were translated for me by a professional translator – a lady who refused to be paid out of respect for the victims of such inhumanity. It was a touching gesture. When I pressed her to accept the payment, she suggested that I could instead make a donation to my favourite charity.

It is a great irony that my mother – who loved all things Italian, spoke the language fluently and even sent an admiring poem to Mussolini in the early days of what seemed then a benign dictatorship – should become a victim of Italy's disastrous alliance with the brutal regime of Adolf Hitler.

Chapter I
'Eva Flatter in Haas'

In September 1994, Viki and I travelled to the Italian city of Arco to meet Professor Maria Luisa Crosina and to visit the memorial she had been instrumental in getting erected. The meeting was a moving occasion – we were joined by several dignitaries from the municipality and we paid our respects by observing a short silence.

On the memorial plaque, my mother's name is inscribed as Eva Haas Flatter, whilst in her book, Professor Crosina uses 'Eva Flatter in Haas' – the Italian equivalent of 'Eva Flatter née Haas'. But it was as Eva Flatter that my mother left Vienna in April 1939. Not having been offered any help from my father to get her out of Austria as she had hoped, my mother thought that it might be easier to rejoin me from Italy.

She wrote to the Italian Consulate for an indefinite permit to stay with her friend Käthe Caliò in Turin. Her application, which included references from respected Italian contacts, was passed on to the Ministry of External Affairs and the Ministry of the Interior. The Prefect of Bozen/Bolzano joined others in support of her application but, to her great disappointment, she was only granted a three-month tourist visa. With that, she travelled first to San Remo and then to Käthe in Turin, who was living there at the time with her husband and first child.

My mother's hope of an early reunion in England received a serious set-back with the declaration of war on Germany by the Allies, following the invasion of Poland, on the 3rd September 1939. By this time she had already over-stayed her three-month visa and was now forced to plead to be allowed to stay longer. This time, in spite of support from the Prefecture of Turin, she was issued with a compulsory travelling order and told that she must leave Italy by the 30th January 1940.

My mother decided to fight back, refusing to resign herself to a return to Vienna and almost certain death. She produced a medical certificate to account for the delay in re-applying and she wrote an impassioned letter in which she said that she would already have left Italy but for the outbreak of war, that her sole aim was to live near her son, and that she was waiting for favourable decisions from the British Consulate in Milan and from Paris to enable her to get to England via France.

Käthe was even more passionate in her cleverly embellished letter of support, addressed to the Ministry of the Interior:

> *Allow me to express clearly and simply the things I feel so deeply and which I so badly need to tell you. It is about my friend, Eva Flatter, who lives with me in Turin. Why will you risk preventing a mother from ever seeing her son again?*
>
> *You must be aware of the conditions under which Jews are now living in Germany, and you must know that it is highly unlikely that my friend will see her son again if she returns to Germany now. In the three years that I have lived in Italy, I have observed that the Italian character is quite free of cruelty. I often think about what Il Duce said about the heart of the Italians. I am also Jewish and I take the things that happened to the Jews as destiny, the unfathomable will of God.*
>
> *I have not lost my loyalty to the Duce as, perhaps, some Jews have, after the proclaimed laws that are unfavourable to them. To be frank, I can admit that I dared write to him about them, being convinced that he is the most just of all Italians.*
>
> *My friend's case is so simple; everyone in Sanremo and in Turin said at first that it would be an easy matter to obtain an extension of the permit. Therefore my friend was in no hurry to obtain a permit to stay in another country beforehand. All at once, around the 15th December, she was told that she could not stay in Italy*

any longer. And we started the procedures for obtaining visas for Switzerland, France and England. We expect that the visa for Switzerland will arrive more quickly than the others, but Switzerland also has its laws and does not send a permit from one day to the next; such a matter always takes 4-6 weeks and they have not yet passed.

I am ready to take an oath under any conditions, that I am giving a true account of the facts. Please permit me to remind you that before Mrs Flatter received the permit to enter Italy, Commendator Limenta, Director of the ELAR in Bolzano, on the request of the Italian Authorities, was able to state that he had made the acquaintance of Mrs Flatter six years ago and gave her an excellent reference as a good and peaceful member of society. I know that my judgment, as a person of no importance, is not worth anything. However, I beg you to allow me to state before the Honourable Minister of Rome, that the Mrs Flatter whom I have known for a long time, is a better and more sincere person than can be imagined. She has already done so much good in her life that deserves consideration.

Finally, I beg you as a mother (I have a two-year-old daughter) for a mother, to be kind enough to allow Mrs Flatter to stay in Turin to await the visa from Switzerland, which will certainly arrive (more quickly than the others, as I have already said) and which is sure to arrive during the month of February, if not sooner.

I am at the disposal of the police and am willing to be imprisoned if what I have said is not true and Mrs Flatter has not left by the end of February <u>at the latest</u> (probably long before then).

A few days ago, my friend Eva Flatter sent a request to your office and I am taking the liberty of supporting her plea. Her son is in England and I hope very much she will not be deprived of the chance of seeing him again.

I ask you again to consider that it is only a matter of a short period of time. If she does not receive a positive reply by the 29th of this month of December, Mrs Flatter will leave for Germany according to the travelling order, which compels her to leave by the 30th of this month if she wishes to avoid arrest.

Yours faithfully

Caterina Caliò, née Perlberg.

In the absence of contrary evidence, it is reasonable to assume that neither my mother's request for an extension of her stay, nor Käthe's supporting letter, would have been answered by the Ministry before the compulsory travelling order came into force on the 30th December 1939. Both letters must have been written after the 15th December and Christmas holidays intervened. The ending of Käthe's letter anticipates this – stating that my mother would leave for Germany if no positive reply is received by 29 December – in the knowledge that she had no intention of returning, preferring instead to become a fugitive within Italy.

With Käthe's help my mother moved to the relative safety of the South Tirol. We know little of her whereabouts until August 1940, but we can be sure that my mother must have abandoned all hope of getting to England during hostilities, when on 10th June 1940, Italy declared war on the Allies. Mussolini, who in 1933 had signed a pact guaranteeing Austria's independence and was then forced in 1938 to condone its annexation by a far more powerful Germany, must have been convinced by the fall of France, Belgium and Holland, to join what he saw as the winning side.

We know from one of Käthe's letters to me, that she, her husband, the two-year-old Anna and my mother, spent a peaceful month in August 1940 in Sarentino/Sarntheim, and that they had to slip away in a hurry because of threats of internment in the newly opened concentration camps for Jews in the South of the country. They went to Rizzolaga in the Province of Trentino.

At this stage, my mother must have felt that she could no longer put her friend and family in danger by her presence. Käthe was herself at risk as a Jewess, but being married to an Italian Catholic and keeping a low profile, she was able to live through the war unharmed. At times, there were people around Käthe who knew that she was

Jewish, but they did not betray her. She always maintained that the anti-Semitic politics of Mussolini were profoundly different from those of the Nazis, and that the Italians were not a cruel people.

My mother moved to the town of Trento/Trent, where she settled down to a modest and retired life, avoiding any attention. However, the authorities caught up with her, and the Prefect of Trent – stating that it was now impossible for her to leave Italy – proposed to intern her within the province, excluding the provincial capital, Trent, and the mixed language (German/Italian) zone.

Her first internment was in Riva del Garda and then in the City of Arco, her final destination before being deported by the Germans. She tried to keep herself by giving lessons and, until 1942, had the help of small sums of money sent to her by my grandmother in Vienna, by a compassionate paternal Aunt Emma in Switzerland and a distant relative in Turkey. Until September that year, she had refused the allowance given to destitute internees, but with my grandmother's deportation from Vienna to Belsen, the departure to the USA of Aunt Emma and the money from Turkey stopped, my mother applied for the allowance, saying she now had no means whatsoever.

In Arco, Eva Flatter was also known as someone who led a very reserved life, but there she was able to rely on the support of two loyal friends: her own doctor and confidant, Dr Ugo Crosina and Mr Carloni, the acting mayor. In describing one of her encounters with my mother, Mrs Carloni vividly recalls a scene which made a painful impression on her:

She once came into the house looking for my husband. She was frightened as if she guessed what was to happen to her before long. I was struck by the fact that she stood in the corridor with her back against the wall. When I introduced her to my husband she did not walk, she <u>shuffled</u> past the walls.

My mother was living on the second floor of a house, which still exists, in Chiarano – a district of Arco. It was surrounded by a large garden and owned by Dr Tommaso Bresciani. Next to the apartment which my mother shared with another family, was that of a Mrs Anna Parolari in Santorum.

To help this *very sweet, shy, reserved woman,* who was in evident financial difficulties, Mrs Santorum had arranged German lessons for her sons at her home. The appointment was on the 21st December 1943 and on the fateful evening of that day, my mother went across to keep it.

They were in the dining room and had barely started the lesson, when there was knocking on the door. Two SS officers stood there. They asked for the Signora. She went with them down the stairs.

After a few days 'the same ones' returned to take her belongings.

So my mother went down the stairs, across the corridor with arches adorned with green arabesques and, passing through the big gate and along the path of the garden crowded with palm trees, she disappeared into the darkness of the winter night.

In the Aliens Register of the Arco Community Archive, Professor Crosina found a short note dated 22nd December 1943. It sums up the tragedy of the day before: *Eva Haas Flatter… put under arrest by the German Authorities.*

My mother was taken to Trent with her companions in misfortune and detained in the via Pilati prison, where Mrs Carloni, on hearing what had happened, went to see her. This very kind lady brought some cake and, as she knew the prison governor as a friend of her father's, was allowed to see my mother, but had to leave the cake at the entrance.

Mrs Carloni reported that Eva was perfectly aware of what to expect. The prison governor told her that this was her only and last chance to see my mother – there would not be another time.

From Trent, my mother was transferred to Fossoli and from there she was deported by rail with Convoy 08, which reached Auschwitz on the 26th February 1944.

That is the last recorded date; after that, there is no further news.

From Professor Crosina's research it emerges that the distinguished author, Primo Levi, was also on Convoy 08. With his account and that of another survivor, Luciana Nissim, it is possible to give an idea of what happened on that terrible night at the concentration and death camp of Birkenau-Auschwitz.

Luciana Nissim describes arriving at night – a deep night – and seeing many vehicle lights which lit an enormous expanse, full of barracks and surrounded by barbed wire. A long line of trucks waited and those who were tired, the old and the sick, and the children, were allowed to scramble on. An SS man looked closely at the women to choose between them – some to the left, some to the right. Then they walked – 29 of them – the others were driven away in the trucks. Eva Flatter was not among them.

Primo Levi also wrote about that scene:

Thus our women, our parents, our children disappeared in an instant, whisked away under our noses; hardly anyone was able to say goodbye to them. We saw them for a short time as a dark mass at the other end of the platform, and then we saw nothing any more.

In 1948, at the request of Benno Haas, his sister Eva Flatter was officially declared dead by the Vienna *Landesgericht* **– the Regional Court.**

Chapter II
Käthe Caliò, née Perlberg

Because she was able to avoid persecution, Käthe does not feature in any of the documents pertaining to the fate of the Jews between 1940 and 1945. Professor Crosina did come across a document in the Eva Haas Flatter file at the Central National Archive, which threw some light on the part Käthe played in helping my mother when she came to Italy. But mainly, the information that fills Professor Crosina's chapter in her book comes from Käthe's letters written to me after the war.

Käthe Perlberg was born in Vienna of a middle-class family. She met my mother when they were students together at the university and they remained friends thereafter. We know that my mother returned to Meran in the *Alto Adige,* the South Tirol, 1935. It is most likely that Käthe was with her then and quite possible that she met Bernado Caliò, a 60-year-old violinist from Sicily, on that occasion. Her marriage to him took place in 1936 and her first daughter, Anna, was born in 1937. Although there was a 30-year age difference between the spouses, the marriage was undoubtedly motivated by love and not by the opportunity to become an Italian citizen.

Käthe had been living in Turin with her husband and little daughter for one year when, in the spring of 1939, she invited my mother to join her. Coming to Turin would rescue her friend from the clutches of the Nazis and provide a base from which she could get to England via France or Switzerland.

It is difficult to establish whether the extreme poverty eventually to befall the Caliò family was partly due to Käthe's concern for my mother, once she was no longer legally in the country. The fact was that they left Turin and moved to the relative safety, but also extreme hardship of life in the South Tirol, in order to hide my mother and, at the same time, to ensure that Käthe herself escaped internment in the newly opened camps for Jews in the South of Italy.

Their stay at Sarentino/Sarntheim is the first recorded by Käthe in a letter to me (The Letters, 30.3.57). It seems to have been almost idyllic, but soon there was an urgent need to move on, to be one step ahead of the authorities. They first settled in the province of Trentino, in Rizzolaga. There my mother decided to face the future on her own. The two friends separated, never to see each other again.

With money running out and a husband incapable of finding work, Käthe tried to find a job as a primary school teacher, but there were two problems: her vulnerability as a Jew and a lack of Italian teaching qualifications. Eventually, she was allowed to teach a handful of mountain farmers' children in Civezzano, a tiny, primitive village in the province of Trentino. The pay was derisory.

By 1943, the family's economic circumstances worsened further. A small allowance Bernado Caliò had been receiving since March 1942 came to an end in April 1943, and there was now another little mouth to feed – a second daughter named Tea.

By all accounts, the country folk around them were very helpful; Bernardo tried to make some money by carving nativity figures and Käthe bartered what she had left of her trousseau. The family was greatly admired for its dignity in the face of poverty; when Tea was born, the neighbours who came to visit found the newborn child lying in the bottom of a suitcase which had to serve as a cradle.

Everyone in the countryside knew that Käthe was Jewish, but no-one broke their silence; on the contrary, the acting mayor replied to an express enquiry from the authorities, dated 18.10.1943, that Civezzano was not harbouring a single Israelite! This compassionate gesture undoubtedly saved Käthe from deportation – the Germans were about to occupy the province of Trentino in the face of crumbling Italian resistance to the Allies advancing from the South.

As soon as the war was over, Käthe tried to make contact with the people she loved, but most were no longer alive to respond. Her mother was deported from Vienna to Poland in 1942; her epileptic sister had died in Terezin/Theresienstadt and Eva...?

In the years after the war, Käthe's life was blighted by ill health, hardship, loneliness and despair but, above all, by an all-consuming guilt for not having saved her dear friend from deportation and certain death. Letter after letter to me was filled with remorse and conveys a feeling that my mother's death had destroyed her life. This is a Käthe dominated by such a powerful, searing thought that it blots out almost all other thoughts or pain:

> *I live here in a tiny little village and have a rather monotonous life. The probable death of your mother has affected me more, and has been more destructive than the probable death of my mother and the certain death of my sister, who died of exhaustion in the infirmary in Theresienstadt. Every day, especially since the end of the war, I relive and feel my guilt afresh.* (The Letters, undated 1946 and 27.1.46.)

In her letters, Käthe says little about her health problems and the hardship of her everyday life. She does complain about the terrible monotony and loneliness of her existence. On one occasion, however, she does mention a mysterious nervous condition she has not been able to shake off, and which is stopping her from reading and writing, whilst also making her indifferent to her misery. (The Letters, 12.9.47)

Professor Crosina remarks in her book that Käthe, besides recalling for me the mother I knew so little, seems also to have had a need to bring her back to life for herself, remembering her character, her weaknesses and her strengths, and always acknowledging her friend's superiority:

> *From every point of view, I am only an intellectually and spiritually weaker imitation of your mother.* (The Letters, 15.4.1946).

I, on the other hand, remember Käthe as an extremely intelligent woman, dedicated to bringing up her children and determined to cope with her harsh life. She shows her caring nature in her letters to me, encouraging me, giving advice and rejoicing at even the smallest success I was able to report. In Civezzano they still think Käthe had a son called Peter!

There is also no doubt that Käthe was a conscientious and totally honest person. According to one account, the family moved to Rovereto in 1947. A bill was still outstanding in Civezzano. The proprietor had forgotten about it by the time he sees, one day, a barefooted woman arriving, her shoes in her hand to save them from wear. It was Käthe, who had come back to pay what she owed.

There is no record of her husband's death, but he was no longer alive when she was in Gaid in 1956. The following year, she was in Vormeswald in the same Val Sarentino where she had spent August of 1940 with my mother. From there she described her life in that impoverished and isolated place in some detail. (The Letters, 30.3.57.)

The girls were growing up and Käthe did everything for them whilst neglecting herself. She continued to teach in spite of poor health and the great problem she had in controlling difficult children. She worked in Caldaro, Appiano Ganda, Merano and San Leonardo in Passiria, in that order, until 1962. In the later years she was joined, as a teacher, by her younger daughter Tea, with whom she had always had a loving relationship.

By 1962 she must have been seriously ill – something she kept from me. She was diagnosed with cancer of the pancreas in the spring of 1964 and had an operation at which the pancreas was by-passed, as it could not be removed. There followed a period of recovery, but by the end of the year, the symptoms returned. Another operation in Switzerland could do little to prolong her life and she died at home on 1st June 1966, after dedicated nursing by Tea, who describes the final stages of the illness in a letter which is full of harrowing detail, but is also imbued with great tenderness towards her mother. (The Letters, Tea Caliò, Meran.)

Käthe's elder daughter Anna married a Pakistani pilot in 1956 and Tea married a *Carabiniere*, an Italian policeman in 1967. They used to return occasionally to Garzano to rediscover their childhood and were last seen there in 1970.

Part IV – The Letters

Letters From My Mother

…I think of you a lot and rejoice over and over again that you are safe…

My father died in 1988. In his safe I found a neatly tied bundle of letters from my mother. I recognised most of them, but not the last two. One of these was dated 22nd August and the final letter, the 25th September 1939, so it must have been a long time coming. Again questions arise: Did my father keep the last two letters from me to avoid another confrontation, or did he want to spare my feelings as war had broken out and correspondence with Italy would soon cease? And why were all the letters in his possession? Had I handed them over to him voluntarily?

Re-reading the letters my mother sent after my arrival in London has been the most painful part of compiling this book. It is clear from the very first letter that she had no conception of my father's latent hatred towards her, nor could she have had any idea of the explosion of rage that greeted me each time I asked him to help her. In the autobiographical Part I, I have tried to find some extenuating reasons for my father's behaviour and for my apparent helplessness. Nevertheless, a strong feeling of guilt for not doing more fills my mind as I read through those desperate pleas for help, written in pencil on scraps of paper. This nagging, ineradicable feeling of guilt is shared by Käthe Caliò, as can be seen from the letters she wrote to me after the war.

Dearest Peter   Vienna 28 September. (1938)

Your letter arrived at last – mine to you had already been sent. It was quite thick, but there was little in it. You could write on both sides of the page, the thick paper won't let it show through. You don't acknowledge my first letter; did the key and the confirmation of your undenominational status arrive??

I see you did well during the journey – no paper bag required? I am glad to hear that you live in green surroundings; that makes it possible to forget the town with all its noise. I can well believe that the town is incredibly big. You write that you are going to a school in the country. Is it always there or is it a safety precaution?

As I have already airmailed a letter to you today, I will close now and continue writing in a few days time. You will get into the habit of answering the questions one by one, won't you!?

Vienna 6 October. (1938)

Your second letter arrived yesterday. It was excessively short, but perhaps you didn't have more time.

Peter, pay careful attention. I will give you an idea of my situation; perhaps Papa can help me with a letter. I have received a third letter from (Comm. Lien?) in which he says that his publisher has experienced a delay, so that the postponement of my journey has not made any difference. I now believe that it would be better for me at the border if I did not mention the possibility of a job, but instead show an invitation from Käte P. who is married to an Italian, in which she asks me to spend a few months at her place and to await an entry visa from England there.

At the same time I would have to have with me a letter from Papa, in which he states that he will shortly obtain an entry visa to England for me, so that I can live near my son and that he will soon advise me at my address in Italy where, he understands, I have been invited.

I have been given this advice by a well-informed official source.

Ask Papa immediately whether he will write this letter for me.

Since Italy is my only chance of finding work, I have to try everything to get there and the letter is only for this purpose.

I cannot postpone the journey further; I would lose the possibility of earning a living. Yesterday I finally settled the problems with the tax authorities and I am supposed to get my passport in the next few days (I applied for it some time ago), so if Omama gives me the money for the fare and Papa sends me the letter, I would be able to travel very soon. In any case, please answer quickly so that I know where I stand.

I am pleased that you are doing well and hope to hear more about it from you. There is nothing new here. Everyone sends greetings, kiss from your mother.

This is my third letter. Did you receive the others? You don't say.

My dear Boy   Vienna (April 1939)

This is probably my last letter from Vienna. I will let you know in case I do not travel. Your answer would come to Omama and would be sent on to me. A few days later you will get a message from me and my address. I don't know it as yet, so don't be impatient, you can imagine that it will take a few days before I know where I can stay for the time being, it is only an experiment. P. (Palestine?) is closed at the moment, I did tell you already, and I cannot remain here either.

Everything alright? Sensible? Fit?

Do you think of me sometimes? I think of you a lot and rejoice over and over again that you are safe, that you don't have to be here.

So you will hear from me next week – earlier if I don't go and probably later if I do.

I will have to be very sparing with stamps and everything, probably later as well, but especially at first which will be an uncertain time. I can hardly send anything to Käthe from here.

So farewell, for now our loving 10. Your mother.

Dear Peter   (San Remo) 27 June (1939)

Have just received your short letter. I cannot turn to Uncle Richard, I believe you when you say he twice asked after me, but he will not help me out with money. When I consulted a lawyer concerning the problem with your departure, who was able to help by getting the tax matter finally settled, I could not say anything about it at home. At that time, when your uncle was already in England, I asked him to help me out with a sum – I believe it was 100 Marks - which I needed to settle the lawyer's bill. He arranged to have this money sent to me from Vienna and I do not think he will do more. He did it then because I had told him it was needed for you – a final attempt to get you out of the country (don't you remember any more how I had to try everything possible, to explore every avenue, until it was settled – to separate yours, that is my tax affairs, from Omama's).

Your letter is not dated, I don't know when it was posted. Could you not have tried something on Sunday in London when you hear it is urgent?

You indicated a few times that you would like to help, that you had a possibility or knew of one. But that does not seem to be the case.

Uncle Richard is also constantly in touch with Else Epst. (Epstein). I prefer to battle on rather than have Omama in Vienna worried, otherwise trouble could grow out of a little help.

That you would leave me in distress, perhaps soon in dire need, in order to avoid difficulties with Papa, hurts me deeply. But I will not write to him, since you believe it will make it bad for you.

One postage stamp here costs 1.25 Lire and not 2 Lire. (The reply coupon comes from Linz, you didn't buy it.)

Tear the letter up. Am staying here, have no money to travel. M.

Dearest Peter   (San Remo) 17 July (1939)

<u>At last</u> a letter from you, I was already worried – is that necessary? Your birthday was on the 5th and you didn't write for almost a week before that and today is the <u>17th</u>.

The whole letter consists of three sentences; you don't explain anything, nothing about America and nothing about anything else. What does it mean that Papa has all his plans in America? I know nothing about it. For all these weeks I was under the impression that you may be coming to a school in Cannes.

You say that I should <u>not</u> write to Papa, and I have not done so, but at the same time you leave me in uncertainty, often you do not write for weeks. I will not ask you about anything any more, I can see it is useless. Do what you will with me.

I already wrote long ago that Käte did not go to Vienna. Her husband went and is still there. When he returns, they will travel together (they only have one passport, I told you) to Vienna for a longer period.

As far as money is concerned, I can expect nothing. Which uncle of Käte's do you mean? The one in America that we talked about quite often has died.

Mother.

Dear Peter (Turin) 22 August (1939)

Received your card yesterday. I could not write because I was ill and without money. I could no longer stay in San Remo, am now in Turin. With her husband and child Käte has one room and a kitchen, so for the time being she has put a settee in the kitchen for me. But they have to vacate the flat on 1st September and I can't stay with them.

I have not written to Papa or to Uncle Richard, I don't find it easy to do, so I waited. Perhaps it would be simpler if you did it. If they sent me something, I could at least go to Milan where there is a Jewish charity providing food and help, I might be easier for me there and I could perhaps find some temporary work because it is a larger town than Turin.

In September I have to get my passport and my visa extended so that I can stay in Italy until I can get away. At the moment Palestine is out of the question and I would not want to go there – I always hoped I would soon be near you. Next month it is one year.

I await your reply *Torino-ferma posta*. Don't hesitate, in a few days time I am homeless. Tear this up.

Mother.

Dearest Peter   (Turin) 25 September (1939)

It is a whole month since I heard from you and I am extremely worried. Three letters from me have produced no reply. I don't even know your address and whether this letter will reach you.

I am in an extremely difficult position because, since the outbreak of war, the passports of Jews are no longer extended here. My passport runs out on 29th September, I have done everything possible including permission to stay in Italy. There is a chance that I will succeed, but I have no money to pay for the passport formalities. I have already sold everything I can manage without.

Please ask Papa if he would, just for once, send me something. I have been living in great need for two months and I am now supposed to be back in Vienna where, according to the local German Consulate, I would be interned because I left illegally.

Or talk to Uncle Richard. Tell him that I am only asking for one single bit of help, it was all so unforeseen.

I was supposed to get some German proof-reading in the autumn, hoped to earn at least enough for essentials, but I can't even travel to Bozen where the written text was, because friends can no longer remain there.

Not hearing from you at all has caused me great worry. Did you receive my letters??

At Omama's there are the same concerns, but she and grandmother are well. Aunt Lise sends me the letters for them and I forward those from Vienna – there is no other possibility. One hears nothing of Uncle Benno; yesterday I sent him a letter from Vienna, from Edith and the children to see if it reaches him via Italy. He is in the African Desert and has been very ill.

Are you with Papa? Or where? What are you doing? Please answer as quickly as possible.

Love, your Mother.

(P.S.) I believe myself to be in Vienna again standing around in offices, just as I was for your tax problems. Do you remember?

Among the many letters received from surviving family members, one from my Uncle Benno and one from Aunt Lisl contain curious assertions. My uncle, having returned to Vienna, writes in 1946 that he cannot understand how my mother could have manage "the extraordinary feat" of giving herself up to the Germans – an assumption negated by the evidence. My aunt writes that she is sorry for what my mother must have suffered, but states: "No, she was not a bad human being, but an unhappy one and difficult to live with." In their different ways, were these manifestations of the survivor's guilt? I wonder!

Letters From Käthe Caliò

Käthe Perlberg was my mother's closest friend going back to student days. She played a major role in the drama that unfolded after my mother had fled Vienna, not only because she initially sheltered her, but also because her letters helped me and Professor Crosina to piece together my mother's movements prior to her arrest in Arco.

Dearest Peter   Garzano di Civezzano 27.1.1946

I have obtained your address through my cousin, who has been living in London since 1939, and also with the help of Richard Flatter. I only saw you as a child and I have often tried to imagine you as an adult. Frequently, during those terrible war years, when I met young men born around 1925, I experienced great emotion at the thought that you too are now grown up.

How are you, dear Peter, and what are you doing, do you have a profession? Sadly, sadly, it is doubtful whether your mother is alive. Do you have any news? I have had none up to now. I know that she was arrested by the Germans at the end of December 1943, that she was imprisoned in Trento for two months and then sent to Fossoli for transportation to Auschwitz on 21.02.1944. After 26.02.1944, there is no further news.

I received this information from the Jewish Committee in Milan and also an address of a lady who was in the same group and had returned to Milan. However, she did not know your mother and could not tell me anything. I have written to the Committee again and am waiting for further news.

Benno has returned to Vienna; Edith is very pleased. Diti died of scarlet fever at the age of 12. Gerda is alive. Your grandmother and my people were all taken away in the autumn of 1942 and there is no further news about any of them.

I am so infinitely sad to think that after suffering so much hardship and mental anguish, your mother may no longer be alive now, when she could have a better life, with you grown up, the joy of seeing you again and so on. I am convinced that your mother was one of the wisest, deepest, richest and unhappiest of human beings of all time. I have met many people, am old enough to understand, to know and to testify. I must confess to you that I feel guilty for letting your mother fall into the clutches of the Germans, I feel that it could perhaps have been avoided if I had had a strong enough impulse to act. But I was lukewarm, passive, undecided at a most critical moment, lacking instinct. If I had conquered a kind of lethargy, a lack of imagination within me, I am sure a possibility such as a secure hiding place would have been my reward. An acquaintance I recently saw again, said he would have hidden your mother. Why did I not search far and wide amongst every possible and impossible, close-by and difficult to reach acquaintances, and ask them, forced them?

In my case, it was unclear from the start whether I would remain unnoticed, but I did. I am not a fatalist, I do not believe in an unalterably ordained fate, but I do believe in pre-determined tendencies and that we come into this world with characteristics which contribute to shape our life. At the same time, I believe in freedom; freedom to fight, to suppress, to avert and, sometimes, to overcome. This battle, the pitiless consequences of the way we think and act, determine our future together with the tendencies given to us in the cradle. I was always very unsure about these questions, but now everything has become clear to me, even though I have expressed it awkwardly.

In the time shortly before her arrest, your mother survived first in Riva and then in Arco, by giving lessons. She was very highly regarded, but also very lonely.

I have two daughters; one is eight and the other three-years-old. I will probably travel to Vienna in the spring. If you have a request, if you need something, provided it is within my powers, I am always there for you. Greet your father and Herr Richard for me.

Very sincerely, Käthe.

Dearest Peter Garzano di Civezzano 15.4.1946

I was so very pleased to receive your kind letter. It moved me greatly and also made me feel infinitely sad. Again, as a thousand times before, I was overcome by guilt, by my horrible heartlessness towards your mother. That you did not get to know her is a loss to you, my poor Peter, of great inner riches, and I fervently hope that you will be at least partially compensate with other experiences in life.

Your father probably has a spiritual and mental narrow mind and may not see certain things <u>at all</u>, does not <u>feel them</u>. I believe you should try, within these limitations, to see and enjoy the good side of his character and to feel a certain gratitude for his love for you. Obviously, you cannot be very fond of him or very close, his coldness, his limitations and his egoism, can hardly be much of a comfort or support.

Would you like to read a German book? I would like to send you one from time to time, especially the ones that your mother liked. Do you know Dostoyevsky? She loved 'The Idiot'.

Your mother sent her diary for safekeeping to Willem van Hoogstraten, a friend with whom she had corresponded for many years. She did not particularly value it, it was sent on an impulse, a friendly thought.

I find it obvious and totally natural that we should address each other by the familiar 'Du'.

Very sincerely, Käthe.

Dearest Peter   undated (1946)

Many thanks for your kind letter. I am very pleased to hear that you are doing well and hope that will continue. I was also glad to hear that your Aunt Lisc has survived the war. Your mother was not in favour of Palestine. I wanted to add to what I have already said about her, that she was never boring. Often even wise and appreciated people can somehow become boring with time, but your mother was always lively, impulsive, full of charm in conversation and in her ideas, which meant that, although she was lonely and troubled, she was never a 'poor dear'.

Quite a number of people wanted to befriend your mother, people who liked her and looked up to her; they were serious and also clever, but they never reached her level, let alone surpassed it. And so it was always your mother who broke off some good relationships, there was no-one amongst these people who could have been a companion, a homecoming for her. She was moody, but not in a silly way. Quite suddenly and without a reason, she could plunge from jovial heartiness into somber, dark and heavy silence; or from detailed participation and over-appreciativeness, into irritability and fault-finding. Perhaps you somehow remember this trait, you too, showed similar signs as a child. It is a rich, but certainly not easy, legacy.

I live here in a tiny little village and have a rather monotonous life. The probable death of your mother has affected me more, and has been more destructive than the probable death of my mother and the certain death of my sister, who died of exhaustion in the infirmary in Theresienstadt. Every day – especially since the end of the war, I relive and feel my guilt afresh.

Your birthday is on the 5th July, you will be twenty-one-years-old. All good wishes, dear Peter, and I send sincere greetings. Käthe.

Dearest Peter   Garzano di Civezzano 20.11.46

I am a little worried not having heard from you. But, of course, it's really my fault. Since writing to you last I have been in a state of suspense. From week to week, month to month, I thought I would at last be able to travel. Bang go my hopes – a new obstacle, a new problem! I finally got my passport, thought I could go, when I am told I must also have a visa from the Allied Authorities in Vienna. More waiting, more uncertainty! God knows, it is not a pleasure trip I am planning; it will be anything but fun.

I would love to have a few lines from you and to know how you are getting on. Are you coming to Vienna? I would so love to see you!

I was prevented from travelling in the summer by illness and lack of money – it might have been easier to get across then. Everything moves so slowly here, as does so much in life. It is despairing that nothing moves, changes, happens. Hopefully, you will have a very eventful life, my dear Peter, with few dead ends. My older daughter is the cleverer, but also a headstrong, cheeky urchin who reminds me of you as a child, when you gave your mother some bitter, sad hours. It must be very satisfying to see one's children finally grown up. How much that is good and has life that you and your mother would have experienced! If you had met as adults, I am sure you would have understood and loved each other.

Sincerest greetings. Käthe.

P.S. Please excuse the scrawl.

Dearest Peter   Garzano di Civezzano 12.9.47

I believe I haven't written to you for a long time. My life is so monotonous here; it seems it was only yesterday that I last wrote. For the past one-and-a-half years I have a nasty, nervous weakness in my head that prevents me almost completely from reading and writing. That is harsh; I am so much more alone and cut off from all that was once dear, near and precious to me. Often, I think it is all a dream; the only thing that will probably maintain my interest and keep me sane, will be my children, although I do not always feel that. My husband is patient, sensitive and understanding, but has a weak nature – no strength radiates from him as, for instance, the immense, convincing strength that was your mother's.

I have written to Salzburg to find out if Hoogstraten is still alive and to ask for his address. So far, no reply, but I will try everything possible to find out if he lives.

There is another possibility that I can go to Vienna, if it does not all end up in frustration as before.

Sincerely, Käthe.

Dearest Peter   Garzano di Civezzano, undated (1947)

Did you receive the letter I recently sent you? I had not written before for so long, because of my poor health and the fact that time seems to stand still here, nothing moves, nothing changes one iota. I hope it is all very different for you. As regards my affairs, I might, just might, receive the visa for Austria, but only for myself, I have to leave husband and children behind.

If you don't want to write, let me at least have a sign of life, whether you are well and in good spirits. If I should get to Vienna after all, I will write from there immediately. Perhaps you will get there before me?

Sincerest greeting, Käthe.

Dearest Peter   Nova Ponente/Deutschnofen 31.12.1949

I am back in Italy, having achieved nothing concrete whatever – the only gain was that my children learned German. Living in a camp was agony at times, but a dear friend from earlier times comforted me. The camp was free and that helped me greatly financially.

Why did you not come to Vienna? I do so want to see you again just the once!! That must surely be possible. I heard that you have married and would hope that you are now less alone! I wish you and your wife every imaginable good fortune!

The diary Eva kept about you does exist. Has Dir. Hoogstraten already sent it to you? I would be so enormously pleased to hear from you once again.

After wandering around in this area for a month with my children, in desperate need and poor health (although the children are always happy), I found a position in a tiny village in the mountains as an elementary schoolteacher (German). I hope to manage for a few years until the girls are grown up.

Sincerely, most sincerely, Käthe.

Dear Peter   (Gaid 1950)

I was really delighted to hear from you. I fervently hope that you will very soon be sufficiently well off to be able to travel with your dear wife. When you have reached that stage, I expect your kind visit with certainty!! It would undoubtedly be interesting for you to see the places of your childhood again.

Everything is now very different in your house in Vienna. The rooms are now austere offices. There was always so much seriousness and solemnity in the house. One can still feel it today, it is a stillness as if there is something outside time in there.

My elder daughter knows and senses much about the past. She always enquires vigorously after you; you are an old acquaintance as if she had already seen you.

Do you have photos of yourself and your wife?

Most sincerely, Käthe.

Dear Peter   Vormeswald 30.3.57

Imagine, I am no longer in Gaid, I was transferred very suddenly and unexpectedly. Where I am now, there are also only eight pupils – until now they had no lessons. Next year, all schools with less than 15 pupils will only get lessons for half a year, meaning that one teacher will serve two schools.

It is possibly even lonelier here than in Gaid. First, one has to travel for three-quarters of an hour by bus from Bozen to Bundschen, and then a two-hour climb up a narrow and very steep woodland path brings one to a group of six mountain farm huts. The forests here are magical and there are huge, strange formations of reddish-grey rock that look as though they would crash down at any moment. The silence is palpable! There are only oil lamps, hens roosting in the kitchen and the people are extremely primitive; but they are people who share all our basic feelings of sorrow and joy.

A person with a strong constitution would suffocate here. Even for a frail person like me, it is perhaps too much of a good thing. I am not troubled by the primitive conditions, but the loneliness makes one a little fearful.

I hope to get a more comfortable post in the autumn. Where we will spend the summer, I do not know, except that it won't be here. In any case, I expect to meet you both in Meran and I will let you know in mid-June where we will be staying.

People here are all wear only traditional costumes – the men and the women. Sarntheim (Italian Sarentino) is the nearest large village. It is the Sarentino in which your mother, my husband and Anna, who was then two-and-a-half-years-old, spent a peaceful August in 1940. We savoured the balsamic air, the beautiful woods, went blueberry picking, stayed in a clean farmhouse and lived on simple food. I can still remember our evening meal of milk and bread. Often, we were quite silent and depressed; the only happy soul was Anna. Your mother would often take her to her room for a time and keep her busy. Anna was restless and somewhat troublesome, but your mother understood so wonderfully how to deal with such a tiny little monkey in a loving and happy way, in spite of her own sorrow and her inborn melancholy.

After a month we had to quickly disappear because of our 'race' and we decided to move to Rizolaga in Trentino province.

Hopefully, you are well and in good spirits. Thea has taken to you and thinks highly of you! Your wife as well, of course. (Anna does not know you yet.)

All best wishes. Most sincerely, Käthe.

Dear Peter   Vormeswald 3.5.1957

Many thanks for your kind letter. As there was no school last Saturday, I took the opportunity to go to Meran and arrived there in the evening. I hope you will be satisfied with the Pension – a rather posh friend of Anna's recommended it. I don't think it's bad, there may be better ones, but I had too little time to find out. What is clear is that the photograph of the place makes it look more splendid than it is.

Meran seems to be quite expensive, it is celebrating a revival. When we were there, Peter, in 1931, Meran was dead, depressingly dead, with a few intellectual, but decadent-tired personalities; today it is once more a spa town through and through. A ritual invasion pours in from Germany, the place is crawling with foreigners. They say that thousands of cars landed in Meran at Easter.

I have reserved a twin-bedded room for you for the 13th and 14th June at L 2500 per day with full board; a single room for me at L 2200 or L 2300. I enclose the leaflet. The 13th should be my first free day, I sincerely hope so. Everything always seems mysteriously to work out for us, don't you think, as last year with our departure. But I must not decry it!

I hope it all works out well and that you will enjoy the holiday. I am looking forward immensely to the 13th and 14th. Best wishes to dear Edna.

Sincerest greetings, your Käthe.

Dear Peter, dear Edna   Rabenstein 2.5.1963

It really is high time for me to thank you for the parcel. We were very, very pleased with it. Unfortunately, we hear nothing from you. The parcel first went to Muthöfe and was then forwarded, and yet I sent you my new address before Christmas or even in the autumn, I can't quite remember. I also sent you a book, dear Peter, and for dear Edna some Marrons Glacés. I hope you received them both.

Tea and I spent the winter diligently learning English. We will probably go away together. But we have children who are as stupid as they are naughty. The landscape is very rugged and beautiful, and totally isolated. Teacher's salaries have just been substantially increased and we are now much better off than hitherto. We have to keep ourselves constantly occupied; otherwise the loneliness bears heavily down. Tea and I spent the winter diligently learning English. We will probably go away for at least 14 days in August, but we do not know where as yet. It would be so nice if your summer holiday brought you near to us again and we could see each other!

All best wishes

Sincerest greetings, your Käthe.

Dear Peter   Rabenstein 4.9.1963

Tea and I were very pleased to hear from you after such a long time, really especially pleased! We had been travelling for two weeks and your letter only reached us yesterday.

We are attending an educational seminar from the 8th to the 14th September. On the evening of the 14th we will already be in Meran and will wait for you there on Sunday the 15th. September is high season in Meran and it is very overcrowded. Please write immediately to the Pension Patria regarding overnight accommodation if you have not already done so.

You are more than welcome to stay with us in Rabenstein; we now have a larger and better apartment than in Gaid. But I don't know whether the path would be too difficult for Edna. Anyhow we can talk about that.

Looking forward to a *Wiedersehen* are Tea and Käthe.

Dear Peter, dear Edna   Rabenstein 21.11.1963

I have often wanted to write, but I am mostly in poor spirits because of the school. Since recently this year, we also teach in the afternoon, but we get Thursday off. Right now, I am sitting in a café in Meran and not thinking about my horrible, stupid, crude louts, with whom I cannot cope. My only hope is that I learn to put up with it, something I don't find easy.

We have had an awful lot of rain. There were some landslides and the road from Riesensteinen was blocked for more than a week. The footpath had disappeared in places. Now the sun is shining and it is not at all cold.

We followed your touchingly caring advice and brought in quite substantial provisions. It is always such a rare and pure joy to spend those few days with you.

The things you bought for us have proved most useful. I am returning your photos with thanks. They have copied well.

I hope you are both well. Many sincere greetings to Edna. And your Käthe greets you especially sincerely. *(Many loving greetings and wishes, your Thea.)*

Letter From Tea Caliò

The last letter from Käthe was followed by an undated letter from her daughter Tea — almost certainly written in June 1966 — announcing her mother's death. It is reproduced here in full and contains a graphic, harrowing account of the suffering her terminally ill mother had to endure.

Dear Peter   Meran

My reason for writing is very sad. My mother died on 1st June. It was an act of mercy because she was suffering so much.

I will report it all because I do not believe you knew about her agonizing illness. Two years ago she was operated in Meran and a pancreatic tumour was discovered. It was not removed, but it was by-passed. She recovered once more and was quite well over the whole of the summer. (Anna was here with her children.) Then, in the autumn, the problems started again with digestive disorders, pain and lack of appetite, which worsened and became unbearable. In the middle of March we decided to do something about it. We travelled to Switzerland where she was operated by one of the best surgeons in Europe, Professor Franz Dencher, in Aarau. He too, could not remove the tumour and they did not know if it was benign or malignant, but there were no metastases present. She was given new by-passes and a part of her stomach was removed.

Before the operation she had only weighed 35 kilos. Now she completely lost her appetite. She was in pain and was given morphine injections. Then she contracted dysentery, which lasted several weeks and completely consumed her. We stayed in Aarau for six weeks.

Then I took her by train and ambulance to Meran, where she stayed in the clinic for three weeks before the doctor discharged her and I nursed her at home for the last two weeks. She was so weak that she could not move in bed on her own – I had to do everything for her. She could only accept liquids and she was given a morphine injection once a day. Her condition was so miserable, she often wished to die. And she knew exactly what was happening to her.

During her last night she was quite normal, as always. She called me a few times to turn her to the other side and she drank some juice. I had a nightmare; I dreamt she had died. When she woke me asking to be turned again, she said, "I had a wonderful dream." I said: "I did not have a nice dream." Then we slept on. At around 5 in the morning, I awoke to hear her groaning. She did not reply when I asked why she was groaning. I gave her some water to drink – her fixed stare was empty and sad. She said, "My mother was so close to me to-night," and she repeated the following sentence four or five times: "My mother was unlucky," and, "You are luckier, you can wake up." Then she slowly slipped away – peacefully, without a struggle and without suffering – I could hardly tell the exact moment.

At last! – after so much suffering. Of course, I am very sad, but I feel that she is now so happy and that comforts me.

Dear Peter, now I will tell you something: firstly please excuse my addressing you with the familiar 'Du', but I feel that it doesn't matter right now because I am writing instead of my mum. Do you know, Peter, that my mother suddenly thought intensely about you during her last days? That is why I am writing in such detail. All of a sudden, she would sob uncontrollably, "Oh dear, now I remember Peter, oh dear, my Peter, how could I forget Peter, why did I neglect Peter so, when he is so close to me , dear Peter, etc."

Due to her weakness she was very sensitive and melancholic. She would say, she would like you to give her a nightdress and then she is shocked because she is only exploiting you. After this she decides that it is not so much a nightdress she wants from you, as a loving thought. (She was wearing the nightdress you bought her in Meran.)

Well, perhaps it's all not so important. It doesn't matter that you didn't write any more – after all, we didn't write to you any more either.

She was buried in Meran on the 3rd of June. Her husband's bones were buried in her grave as she had once wished. I wrote to Anna's husband and sent the letter to a friend in Pindi, so that the news will be gently broken to Anna. She is expecting her third child in July, which is why we kept things from her.

I am engaged to an Italian, a *Carabiniere*. He is unsophisticated, but very kind and loving (thank God, otherwise I would be completely lost).

Dear Peter and Edna, I would like to see you both soon. Come when you feel like it and when it's convenient. We live (that is now: I live) in Meran for the past one-and-a-half years in an attractive modern apartment. You can stay here any time and eat here. Mum often wished it; she thought Edna would really feel at home in our apartment.

Dear Peter, dear Edna, don't be too sad; I am not that sad either, because I sense that my mother is so happy.

All loving thoughts, your Tea.

Anna took her mother's death badly. She had her third child in July 1966. Tea married her Carabiniere in August 1967 and they went to live in Postal/Burgstall, near Meran.

The Guilt Of The Survivor – A Postscript

...mach mit mir, was du willst – do with me, what you will...

...these are not words of resignation, they are written in anger by a desperate mother accusing her son of not helping her and they made a 13-year-old boy feel guilty for the rest of his life.

Guilt seems to run through the pages of this book, but examples of compassion feature too. In fact, a few apparently inconspicuous examples blaze a trail of human kindness amidst events of utter inhumanity: the people of Civezzano who did not betray Käthe, the mayor who committed perjury for her, the lady who went all the way to visit my mother in Trent prison and brought a cake for her. There is Professor Crosina's dedication in recording the fate of Jews in Northern Italy which goes far beyond academic involvement, and the translator who refused payment as a gesture of support for her work...! But, above all, guilt in various guises dominates the story.

In his book 'Lloyd George, Woodrow Wilson and the Guilt of Germany', Dr A Lentin describes the struggle between the leaders of the Western Allies when formulating the terms of The Treaty of Versailles, following WWI. Woodrow Wilson's strong opposition to calls for retribution – most firmly demanded by the French – did not win the day, as Lloyd George was faced with placating a revenge-thirsty public in Britain and could not support a more moderate approach. As a result, the guilt of Germany for the war and its slaughter became the basis of the Treaty. To what extent, if at all, Versailles was subsequently instrumental in creating WWII, appears to be a matter of controversy among historians, but there is no doubt that in 1919, the entire population of Germany was punished and felt humiliated. Ironically, the harsh terms meted out to the Germans generated feelings of remorse in Britain, a sentiment which is said to have contributed, in the 1930s, to the British Government's policy of appeasement – an unfortunate reluctance to stop Hitler in his tracks.

We know that guilt played a very different role in WWII. The Allies set out to punish only those directly guilty of war crimes and crimes against humanity, whilst the German people as a whole were helped to rebuild their economy within a democratic state.

This left Germans to make up their own minds as to how much they shared in the guilt of their leaders. They had supported a movement that grew from small, brutal beginnings into a human disaster of cataclysmic proportions, and they could hardly blame more than its genesis on the Treaty of Versailles.

At first, travelling in Germany, one heard a lot of "I was always against it", with a minority still justifying Hitler's actions and avowing posthumous allegiance to the 'Führer'. Little or nothing was taught in schools about the Nazi era for quite a long time. But with new generations came a potent legacy of guilt and a strong desire to make amends.

My erstwhile Austrian fellow countrymen, who had embraced National Socialism even more enthusiastically than their German neighbours, declared themselves victims and refused, for many years, to accept any guilt for their part in the disaster. It took a second generation to begin what were initially reluctant moves to acknowledge responsibility for what had happened. It is not to the credit of successive Austrian governments, that restitution payments to victims were delayed for so long, that a large proportion of the survivors were no longer alive to receive them.

The manifestations of guilt that mark my story, started with my failure to make an unsympathetic father listen to my mother's plight, or to persuade him to help her in any way whatever. The letters she wrote me assumed that I was not even trying. They made me feel helpless, powerless and, ultimately, guilty. Did I do enough to persuade my unbending father to get his former wife to safety? Should I have tried other possibilities? Was I cowardly, selfish, unfeeling?

But worse: following my mother's death, Käthe Caliò tortured herself for the remainder of her life with the conviction that she could have saved her dear friend from deportation – an obsession that ultimately destroyed her.

And then there is another kind of guilt – the guilt of the survivor for having survived. Writing and compiling this book has made me relive much of what has happened and has also compelled me to imagine the suffering of the victims. As a picture emerges in my mind of my mother being herded into a cattle truck, forced to stand during the two-day nightmare journey to Auschwitz and arriving there in such a weak condition that she would immediately be selected for the 'showers'; stripped naked and finally slowly, painfully choked to death, alone and abandoned amidst the unimaginable terror of the gas chamber – I ask myself the question: why was I spared, what entitles me to lead this charmed life of mine? And then I think: what can I do to somehow 'atone' for my good fortune?

Perhaps the answer to the last question is: I can at least record my mother's tragic fate in the hope that together with thousands of other not-so-different stories, it can touch hearts and keep this abominable example of man's cruelty to man alive in the minds of future generations.